ISLAMIC ARCHITECTURE
AND ITS DECORATION

TABRIZ

Tilework in the courtyard of the so-called Blue Mosque
A.D. 1465

ISLAMIC ARCHITECTURE
AND ITS DECORATION
A.D. 800-1500

A Photographic Survey

by

DEREK HILL

With an

Introductory Text

by

OLEG GRABAR

THE UNIVERSITY OF CHICAGO PRESS

THE UNIVERSITY OF CHICAGO PRESS
CHICAGO 37

FABER AND FABER LIMITED
LONDON WC 1

Published 1964

Printed in Great Britain by
R. MacLehose and Company Limited
The University Press Glasgow

CONTENTS

7

ILLUSTRATIONS

COLOURED PLATES

MONOCHROME PLATES

(All the following plates are at the end of the book)

9

ILLUSTRATIONS

There is a map of the areas covered on pages 24 and 25

ACKNOWLEDGMENTS

First my thanks are due to Mrs. Joan Taylor for her splendid work in enlarging nearly five hundred photographs. Whatever merits these may have I feel the responsibility is largely hers.

I would also like to thank the Turkish Government and Tourist Board for facilitating the three journeys made to their country. On the first journey my gratitude went as well to Mrs. Freya Stark who accompanied me, and on the second journey to Bay Akşit Gökturk of Istanbul University, an able guide, interpreter and friend. The third journey was shared partially with Rear Admiral Paul Furse and Mr. Patrick Synge, both on an official botanical 'mission' from the Royal Horticultural Society. They nobly agreed to countless deviations of aim when Islamic architectural remains were nearby.

Great kindness and consideration were shown by the Intourist office in Samarkand and through this body I was able, with the help of Mr. Anvar Karimov, to obtain photographs from the Committee, in Tashkent, responsible for the preservation of early Islamic monuments in Russian Central Asia. Also, through the continued perseverance on the part of Mr. Viktor Schnittke the Photographic Archive of the Scientific Research Museum of Construction and Architecture in Moscow gave me invaluable data on buildings I had not been able to visit for myself. Finally, the staff of Faber & Faber have courageously persevered over a difficult task.

Beyond these acknowledged tokens of gratitude I can never forget the countless friends who, both at home and abroad, helped to fulfil the object of these ten years' journeyings. To them and to the friends who were able to fill in gaps in the photographic material this book is dedicated and to the memory of Bernard Berenson which has been my chief source of inspiration during the period of research.

D. H.

The author and publishers acknowledge with thanks the receipt of a generous grant from the Gulbenkian Foundation towards the cost of producing this book.

A LETTER TO DEREK HILL
FROM BERNARD BERENSON

I TATTI, 1958

Dear Derek,

I congratulate you on having seen so many cities of inner Asia Minor and thank you for the beautiful photographs you took of the Seljuk buildings you saw, admired and now communicate to us, your readers.

What a miracle is this Seljuk architecture! It has an elegance, a distinction of design and a subtle delicacy of ornament surpassing any other known to me since French Gothic at its best. No doubt it owes much to the nature of the stone at its command that could yield a masonry of almost jewel-like precision. For composition, mass and structural design it owed something to the Armenized Byzantine style, for the dome-like buildings to Constantinople alone. Yet influences count for little where there is no genius to be affected. Look at the muddiness of Armenian ornament compared with Seljuk, although both used the same kind of stone.

One cannot help asking where this gifted people came from, where their genius for art matured. We are led to think of the sandburied cities of the Lop Nor, of Turfan for instance, and the gorgeous mural and Manichean miniature painting done there and of its Turchi descendants, in their turn the precursors of earliest Persian illumination.

I have been only to Konya among the cities that you visited, and Konya was the residence of the Seljuk rulers and is still an unrivalled monument to their taste and their love of beauty and magnificence. They were enlightened and their orthodoxy was challenged by the Islamic clergy. For good reasons. Intermarried with the court of Constantinople they had connections even with far-off Germany.

The early XIIIth century in Asia Minor was an age of chivalry, of continuous tournaments between Christian and Muslim. It was the age of Akrites, the Byzantine parallel to the Spanish Cid. It was an age that produced the glamorous romance of Sharkan and Abriza embodied in the Arabian Nights. No religious fanaticism or merely expletive, like so many of our swear words.

13

A Letter to Derek Hill from Bernard Berenson

Everything helped the Seljuk miracle. Seljuk art inspired what was best in Ottoman architecture as we still see it in Brussa, and in the mosques outside Mylas, at Ephesus and at Miletus.

I am delighted to find among your reproductions several of the 'Sultan Hans' that the Seljuk rulers built all over their possessions. Like the Hellenistic Basilicas they were royal structures, to serve as caravanserais, with a central building consisting of a nave and two aisles, not unlike Italian Gothic or the Crusaders' cathedral at Tortosa, and a small mosque decorated with exquisite ornament in the courtyard. These Hans are a prominent feature of Seljuk architecture. We drove out about a hundred kilometres from Konya to see one of them. Far away on the horizon was a snowy mountain and I was filled with longing to go there and beyond; but to write about that would be a chapter of my autobiography, related to your evocative pictures in so far as it is through looking at them and reading your excellent commentaries that I feel in a nostalgic mood. May your book have the same effect on many of your readers.

BERNARD BERENSON

PREFACE TO THE PHOTOGRAPHY

by Derek Hill

It is natural that since I am a painter my primary interest in the decorative features of the architecture I have photographed should be aesthetic.

Fortunately Professor Oleg Grabar undertook with enthusiasm the erudite task of putting order to the data I had collected over the last ten years and was able to give an historical survey and scholarly captioning to what would otherwise be a mere collection of photographs. As he points out, the area I have photographed and the period concerned are far from inclusive of the whole vast field of Muslim architecture. Other countries from the ones shown here, such as Spain, India and Egypt, have been fully dealt with in other books — so have the later periods of architecture even in the countries here represented. The whole enterprise started, on my part, with a desire to record examples of decoration in architecture necessary to bring to life a blank wall: also the proportion of decoration needed on the given blank space to ensure the maximum impact. This interest originated from being shown, when still a schoolboy, the photographs and drawings that Robert Byron had brought back from his 'Road to Oxiana' journeys and from reading the books of Adrian Stokes, with his absorption in the 'flowering stone' of architecture. From these beginnings the interest had widened to include the theories of Matyla Ghyka on the influence of nature and natural objects on architecture and its proportions, and, through the ensuing study of the laws of harmony and the divine, or golden, section, to a realization of the intimate connections between music and architecture (or 'frozen music' as Ghyka calls it). In painting of course these various connections are just as valid, and the construction of a picture, of any period, should be equally concerned with proportion, harmony and music as the construction of a building. Countless examples of artists referring to the similarity or necessity of 'music' to their work exist throughout the ages down to Van Gogh, Braque and Pasmore in our own days. Braque has even included the name J. S. Bach on one of his collages and by doing so has given 'music', a decorative note, to an otherwise formal and arid composition.

This name of Bach printed across a picture has the same telling power that the Kufic lettering has on the otherwise plain brick surface of the Gunbadh-i Qabus, as an example. It succeeds in bringing to life the entire work of art or of architecture. The only difference between the two is the 900 years that elapse — not the intention. Today however architecture seems to be more concerned with shape than with life-giving decoration. The Gunbadh-i Qabus, a strangely pencil-like mausoleum rising out of the flat steppes that border Russia and Persia on their Caspian Sea frontier, combines, most successfully, the two. That I feel sure is why Robert Byron wrote that 'the Gunbadh-i Qabus ranks with the great buildings of the world'.

Ten years ago it had been the pointed towers (not unlike, and perhaps influencing, the Gunbadh-i Qabus) of Armenian architecture in Turkey that had made me try to reach the island of Agthamar on Lake Van and the ruins of Ani above the stream that separates Russia from Turkey. In both places could be seen the marvellous assimilation of stone cutting and carving used by the ninth- and tenth-century architects. Unfortunately, owing to political and territorial obstacles neither goal was reached, but various similar Armenian buildings along the route were seen which excited interest for the same reason. Also for the first time I saw the architecture left by the Seljuqs, descendants of the first Turkish tribe from the region around Lake Baikal to cross the deserts and settle in Anatolia.

The Seljuqs had already adopted the Muslim religion in the tenth century but had certainly felt the influence of the Christian Armenian architecture that they had met with on their migrations; the Armenians in their turn being equally influenced by Byzantium. Also the Sasanian architecture, of which now practically nothing remains, must have influenced the Seljuqs on their arrival in Persia before continuing west into Anatolia. In spite however of these influences, with possibly a surmised one from China, through the Ghaznavid empire in what is now Afghanistan, they managed to produce an architecture as noble and enduring in its impact as any that we know, and also as original. The earlier the architecture left by these various groups of semi-settled nomads the better it is — the simpler and the more effective — and its final burst of grandeur, before decadence, seems to have been under Tamerlane, who produced a true conqueror's architecture, following along the same lines as the earlier invaders. Already by the time of Gawhar Shad, Tamerlane's daughter-in-law, the element of decoration for decoration's sake seems to be in control and the herbaceous border from a merchant's seed packet has ousted the more severe and formal lay-out. Robert Byron felt that Gawhar Shad's buildings were the summit of achievement but unfortunately he never crossed the Oxus

16

Part of the tiled dome, in turquoise and purple, of the Karatay Madras'ah at Konya.

The effect is very like the flowers of a thistle (see below)

Thistles photographed in Turkey, near Konya

Decoration at corner of a walled up archway at
Nisibin, near the church of St. James

A desert plant giving life to the flat surface of the ground

to see Samarkand or Shahr-i Sabz. Gawhar Shad and her multi-coloured tile work already foreshadowed the decorative arabesques of Shah Abbas in Isfahan and the Moghuls in India. If the courtyard of Gawhar Shad's mosque in Mashhad is like a flower garden the earlier tile work with its geometrical patterns (even the Kufic writing was coerced into this geometry) is more like a bed of thistles or the thorny succulents that one finds in desert places. During their great migrations across the deserts of Central Asia the few signs of plant life must have seemed like manna to these tribes and it would be no wonder if they showed their gratitude by adapting to their architectural decoration the patterns they found in these testimonials of life. Similarly the blue of the early tiles is the blue of the 'rollers', the birds that so often provide the only touch of colour on those sandy plains. The pointed roofs of their mausoleums may, if they are not derived from the similar roofs of Armenian churches which could well in their turn have the same source, come from the pointed tents of the tribes. Or they may with their tiled surface represent the blue sky to the furrowed brick work of the land beneath. The more one sees of this architecture the more convinced one becomes that natural objects have been the inspiration for all decoration — and this is true down to the later periods when pottery, materials, rugs and walls all had their covering of floral tributes.

This later tendency to overall decoration was in direct contrast to the rigid simplicity of a building like the Gunbadh-i Qabus or the Arslan Jadhib mausoleum at Sangbast near Mashhad. The two styles are as far apart as Strawberry Hill Gothic and early Norman. One style relies on an outward and showy abundance and the other on an ordered and proportioned harmony. The periods at which this more restrained perfection has been achieved are all too rare. Renaissance architecture had it and architects like Alberti, Brunelleschi, Francesco di Giorgio and Laurana — to name only the leaders — knew precisely where to put their 'pietra serena' ornament to make it most telling. Also they knew just how much of the 'pietra serena' to use on the plain surface to give it life. English silversmiths of the seventeenth and eighteenth centuries had the same impeccable knowledge and so did the best of the French 'ébénistes' at the end of the eighteenth century. On the furniture of Saunier and of Weisweiler one finds exactly the correct amount of ormolu used in the design and it is only when these craftsmen were given elaborate orders by an over-rich court that their natural sense of proportion came to grief and Sèvres plaques and finicky veneer ruined the otherwise excellent good sense. For good sense is really what this desirable instinct consists of. It has the same control on over-elaboration that a good chef should have, a good dressmaker, or a good jeweller. For the perfect menu a complicated and rich dish should be preceded and followed by courses of the utmost simplicity. The plain fare demands just as much attention as the rich one, if not more; it is merely that the one complements the other. Today the seemingly inevitable slab-cake buildings that grow daily in every city have gone to an extreme where no decoration or elaboration of any kind is allowed. Perhaps they do come to life for a short period at twilight when lights go on and office workers have not yet left for home. There is so often little or no attempt to break up a dull, dead flat surface by even some simple decorative device that can give it life: the 'stone flowering' that Adrian Stokes writes of. In interiors the same lack is everywhere evident and it is here that contemporary painting of the 'Blot and Diagram' variety, as Sir Kenneth Clark describes it, comes into play. Whether the artist so intends or not, his doubtless agonized work of self-expression simply provides the much needed animation to a plain wall that so many modern architects are entirely incapable of giving. A great deal of this useful painting is less a symptom of our age than an architectural need — something born of necessity, in the same way that patterned tiles were discovered at a moment when they were needed to flower upon unembellished walls. An early page of the Koran is as beautiful as say a *graffito* drawing by Mathieu (purely aesthetically; as one is functional and the other is mere decoration). There is no point in citing further examples as it simply becomes a snobbish game of erudition. Unfortunately the paramount difference between all these examples that could so easily be given is that the craftsmen of a thousand years ago worked towards some definite goal — the completion of the Koran in honour of Allah, of a mausoleum in honour of their family or some such worthy object. Today the modern artist often fails when any commission for a modern decoration is given in that he simply works for himself by himself and within himself — however much he may deny this. Coventry cathedral is the perfect example of this failure. It is not that too many cooks have spoiled the broth, merely that each cook has produced his best dish and the resulting menu does not add up to a well chosen meal. Similar examples can certainly be found among these photographs. The great mosque at Divrig is over elaborate and unharmonious to an almost ludicrous degree. The western Crusade-influenced 'rose' window of the Sunghur bey mosque at Niğde certainly does not go with the rest of the solely Islamic building. However in the most successful buildings within this present survey there is a harmony and completeness that cannot be criticized, and which allow the construction to take its place with the finest achievements of ancient Greece, Gothic France and England or Renaissance Italy, or, as Robert Byron puts it more simply,

18

the great buildings of the world. Through earthquakes and natural phenomena, not to mention invasion and wars, these masterpieces are in daily danger of destruction and it seems to me little short of a miracle that so many have survived, often in comparatively good condition. However, it is time that some photographic record of what still remains should be kept.

Unfortunately many of the photographs can be criticized in that they do not give as often as I should like the contrast between the decoration and the undecorated surface around. The difficulty of giving within two dimensions the proportions in both decorated surface and undecorated on an entire building seems insurmountable and a mere approximation is all that is possible.

In this book will however be found examples of all the important ornamental decorations used on Islamic architecture within the defined regions of Asia, from a period that has, in this decoration, most bearing upon our own.

Apart from the use it may have for scholars a collection of photographs of ornamental details from this comparatively little known part of the world could provide for architects a fund of inspiration that they could adopt for bringing back to architecture a neglected but integral part of it. Many young architects of today, in fact, have already started a search for decorative features that they can incorporate into their buildings. Variations of brick work and even tile work are among the things they have tried and I hope they may get help from this presentation as they have from the designs of William Morris and De Morgan. As de Falla said: 'Poor are those who blinded by the brilliant new art reject the old one. They miss voluntarily great and exquisite pleasures which raise the pleasure produced by the modern art by discovering in it the more or less direct consequences of the old one.' De Falla was thinking of music; he could have been thinking of painting or architecture, and at a period when, probably as never before, examples of art from the past have little or no interest for or influence on, the so called creators of today. As in Constable's day 'a self taught artist is one taught by a very ignorant man.'

ISLAMIC ARCHITECTURE
AND ITS DECORATION

The value of this volume lies in its plates. For the first time there have been assembled general views and characteristic details of Islamic architecture which are not tied to specific national, ethnic, or geographical entities; nor are they so few in numbers as to be almost meaningless for any sort of generalization concerning so vast a world as that of the Muslims. The central aim of these photographs has not been to reproduce all aspects of a rich architecture, but to capture something of the nature of Islamic architectural decoration. This aim is not the result of an idle attempt at an old-fashioned grammar of ornament nor does it derive from a mere fascination with detail for detail's sake. It has rather two distinct and yet complementary causes. On the one hand, while technical and spatial problems have occupied much of the energy of contemporary architecture, an interest in and a need for means to articulate, emphasize, or alleviate wall spaces through ornament has always existed and has recently again been brought out in architectural discussions; hence any presentation of early solutions to ornamental problems may be of value to modern architects or to laymen. On the other hand, it is a peculiarity of Islamic art that, at a certain period in its evolution and for reasons to be presently defined, a fascination with the infinite variations which can be given to wall surfaces took precedence over other architectural considerations. It will be one of the aims of this introduction to describe and evaluate the results of this fascination.

At the same time neither the photographs nor the introduction should be construed as covering the whole of Islamic art. The monuments of Cordova and Granada in Spain, of Rabat and Marrakesh in Morocco, of Kairouan in Tunisia, the justly celebrated masterpieces of Cairo, Jerusalem, or Damascus, the almost magical creations of the powerful Ottoman, Safavid, and Mughal empires of the sixteenth and seventeenth centuries — such as the mosques of Istanbul, the *masjid-i shah* of Isfahan, or the Taj Mahal — all these and many other Islamic monuments are missing. For the collection to be presented here, with a few exceptions, belongs to a fairly well delineated time, the eleventh to fifteenth centuries, and to a rather peculiar geographical area. This choice of dates and regions can be justified on historical and cultural grounds, and with a few exceptions either impossible or difficult to reach, the most important monuments of the time are here included.

A constant problem of Orientalism is to decide how to transliterate names of people and places; the problem is compounded in this instance because Turkish, Iranian, or Arabic versions of the same word will be found and it would obviously be silly to use *khān* when a caravanseraglio is in Persia or Syria and *han* when it is in Turkey. Hence we have eliminated all diacritical marks on place names and on the names of monuments and given them the spelling presently used in such countries as use Roman letters or a simplified transliteration which should not prevent those who know the languages from putting the words back in their original shape. We have used the *Encyclopedia of Islam*'s system of transliteration (with two changes: *j* instead of *dj* and *q* instead of *ḳ*) for technical terms.

I. SPACE AND TIME, PEOPLE AND PURPOSES

1. THE PHYSICAL SETTING

The area which harbours most of the monuments reproduced here could be defined as a long trail which begins uncertainly between the Aral Sea, Lake Balkash, and the western tip of the Tienshan Mountains. Cutting across deserts and river valleys, it moves southwards or south-westwards in the direction of the Iranian plateau; it crosses the Elburz chain near Nishapur, follows the mountain range on its south side, then splits into two parts, a northern one through the intricacies of the Armenian knot and a southern one through northern Mesopotamia; both ways meet in the central Anatolian plateau where the trail ends. From this main trek secondary routes branch out. They vary in character. In Central Asia, between the Caspian Sea and the Pamirs, like an inkblot, our track follows up and down the valleys of the Oxus, the Jaxartes, the Zerafshan, until it is stopped by high mountains in the east, deserts and the Caspian Sea to the west. As it reaches the north-eastern corner of the Persian plateau — the area of Rayy to Qazvin — a part of it suddenly shifts southward toward Isfahan, Shiraz, and Kerman, the ancient province of Fars, with its Achaemenid and Sasanian memories and the newer province of Jibal covering the mountains of the Zagros and the high plain bordering the great central desert. From there a secondary trail descends into the hot and rich Tigris and Euphrates valleys and reaches Basrah or Baghdad, where this secondary route ends at the edge of the Arabian desert. Since very few medieval monuments remain from lower Iraq, it is not represented in our survey.

If we return again to the Qazvin region, we can follow the trail in two separate ways. The northern one through Tabriz and Erzerum also extended a branch northward beyond the Araxes to Christian Georgia and especially along the Caspian coast all the way to Derbend. The area of northern Azerbayjan, little known and difficult of access, could not be fully covered in this volume, even though it contains very important remains of medieval times. The southern road followed the northernmost part of the Fertile Crescent, in full view of the mountains of Anatolia and of the steppe and desert land that, crossed by few rivers, carries its alternately flat and tormented majesty down to the Indian Ocean. From this southern road also secondary tracks broke off, down the Tigris to Mosul and Baghdad, down the Euphrates to Rahbah and Anah, or toward Damascus, Jerusalem, and finally Egypt, where another desert separated the truly Near Eastern Islamic world from the Western one.

Although not all the branches and parts of this trail have had the same historical development, the trail itself is not an artificial creation, but a geographically definable area. Physically it is characterized by the almost constant presence of high and almost inaccessible mountains, of deserts, and of cultivated land, or, more correctly, of land susceptible of cultivation. Desert and cultivated land are, of course, historically variable terms; a desert in one century can become a significant agricultural area in another period, the variations depending on the degree to which available water is used. The techniques for the use of water varied considerably also. In Mesopotamia or in Central Asia much land could be conquered from the desert for agricultural purposes whenever the rivers were used for irrigation. In west-central Iran it was first the discovery of water deep under the earth and then the transportation of the water through underground channels that could give prosperity to the districts bordering the central desert. What this means then is that the obvious physical traits of an area today do not of themselves determine the character of the area in the past. Much of Central Asia and of northern Mesopotamia was, in the middle of the nineteenth century, almost desert, with a few oases for weary and frightened travellers; it could then hardly be imagined that a highly developed agriculture and an extensive and comparatively safe trade had characterized northern Mesopotamia in the second millennium B.C., or Central Asia shortly before the Muslim conquest.

23

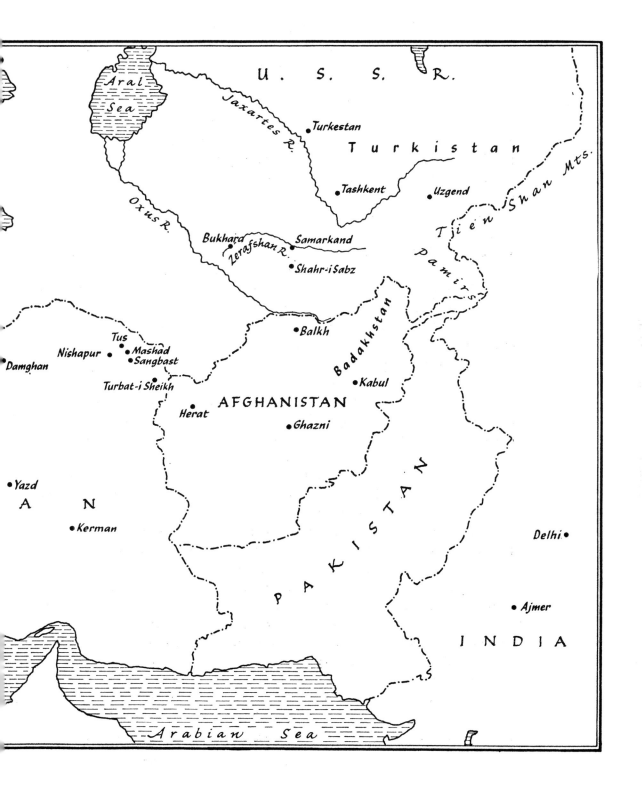

To a very large extent human factors determined the character of these regions; and, from the necessary emphasis on problems of the use and conservation of water rather than from reliance on natural rainfall which characterizes almost every part of this world, it is clear that the permanence and wealth of settlements were dependent on the working condition of their water systems. Hence the central feature which could 'make or break' any province was the existence or lack of security from professional bandits, desert nomads, or wild mountaineers. But, even though they could be held in check, desert nomads or mountain people could never be eliminated, since regions totally unfit for settled habitation and inaccessible mountain areas were unchangeable parts of the landscape. Thus it is that the physical character of this vast area has imposed on it a tension between opposing interests and aims which can best be defined in the human terms of a struggle between the desert and the sown, the highland and the lowland, a struggle in which, paradoxically enough, the existence of the wealthy and settled agricultural community is far more essential to the livelihood of the roving nomad or to the mountaineer than the other way around. The only significant use the nomad has ever served for the settler has been to protect him against other nomads, an activity which has been at the root of many a dynasty.

There is yet another basically geographical dimension of the area. It is an area of movement, of passage. There are two aspects of this dimension. On the one hand it means that the zone was one of trade, i.e., one through which goods, men, and ideas moved back and forth. Around commerce and commercial activities there grew a whole apparatus of service organizations, from the caravanseraglios in which the caravans stopped, to the shops, places for entertainment, restaurants, barbershops, hospitals and cemeteries, in which the travellers could and did receive necessary — and sometimes final — services. But, on the other hand, this zone was also a zone of invasions. It is through there that, at some obscure moment in the middle of the second millennium B.C., Indo-Aryan tribes apparently transformed the Iranian plateau into an Indo-European enclave and pushed all the way to northern Mesopotamia. Early in the first millennium the same route was taken by the Iranians whose various groups, from the Soghdians in the north-east to the Persians proper and the Medes in the west and south-west, occupied the rest of Iran. It is through these same ways that the Achaemenid empire extended itself into Anatolia and Egypt. And it is along the same way — with only minor differences — that Alexander the Great moved eastward. A few centuries later the Parthians struck the Roman empire following in the footsteps of earlier armies. This characteristic of our area as a perennial passageway for armies and whole peoples from East to West and, more rarely, from West to East could not but affect its human, ethnic, and even physical character. Much in its economic life was precarious; its cities were often destroyed. Yet here also there lies a paradox, for all these movements also created wealth, and the destroyed towns were, most often, rebuilt. Its being a passageway led both to the prosperity of this area and to the constant disasters which afflicted it.

It is, of course, true that any more detailed analysis will discover considerable differences between the various parts of the huge zone we are trying to describe. Deserts and mountains may be present everywhere, roaming desert nomads or frightening mountaineers may be lurking on the way of caravans or may be following from afar the slow march of invading armies from the passes of Anatolia to the Tienshan Mountains. Yet, at the very same time, other geographical and human criteria clearly permit one to distinguish certain provinces from others. Our choice in identifying them lies between using modern or medieval divisions of the land. If we have preferred the latter, it is because they do correspond much better than do contemporary national boundaries to the people and events which created the monuments shown on the plates.

To the extreme north-east was the ill-defined province of *Ma-wara-an-nahr*, literally 'what is beyond the river', i.e., Transoxiana. This generic term embraced all lands between the Oxus and the fully nomadic steppes and deserts of the north. Transoxiana comprised several parts, whose histories and destinies varied considerably: the mountains of Badakhashan, rich in minerals, with magnificent pastures and the road to Tibet; Tokharistan, a strange province, whose major centre was south of the Oxus in the great city of Balkh-Bactria the 'Mother of Cities', on the main routes from Central Asia to India, but whose agricultural wealth was derived from towns and villages along rivers flowing straight south toward the Oxus; and it is almost at the confluence of one of these rivers with the Oxus that we find the ruins of Tirmidh, one of the great cities of medieval times, from which extraordinary stuccoes have been uncovered in recent decades. Farther north across the Pamir was the province of Ferghanah, where the Jaxartes began. It was a rich province during much of the Middle Ages, for it was at the Near Eastern end of the road to China through the Tarim basin and thus the centre of a lively trade whose fluctuations depended on the complex developments taking place on the western frontiers of China. But perhaps the most important factor of Ferghanah's prosperity was that, after 751 when the last Tang or Tang-supported armies left, its position to the side of the main route of invasions made it more secure from devastations

27

than most other parts of Central Asia. Of the middle and lower courses of the Jaxartes little is known; in the early Middle Ages this was an insecure and dangerous area, and it was only in the tenth century that major Muslim cities began to appear not merely on the river itself but, like Taraz (Talas), beyond the river in Semirechya, the province of the seven rivers and one of the first centres of Turkish power.

The frightening Red Desert (Kizil Kum) separates the Jaxartes from the Oxus except at the north-west and the south-east. In the north-west, a short, if perilous, road connected the Jaxartes with the ancient province of Khorezm, whose brilliant past has only recently been discovered. To the south-west the provinces of Ushrusanah and Soghd and the valley of the Zerafshan served as a tie between Ferghanah and the road to China, the northern road to Siberia, the south-eastern road to Balkh and India and, finally, the road to Iran. This position at the crossroads of Asia and the existence there of good water supplies gave the cities of Bukhara and Samarkand an agricultural and commercial basis as well as a mysterious and expensive aura which enthralled the imagination of Shakespeare as well as of the Russian and British officers who lived and died there for the great imperial battles of the nineteenth century. It is also their position which made these cities vulnerable to foreign invaders, and few towns have had an equally chequered succession of rulers.

As one crosses the Oxus from the north, the huge province of Khorasan extends almost from the Caspian Sea to the Hindu Kush. Geographically the area is not a clearly defined one, except from the point of view of those who coined the term, i.e., the pre-Islamic Persian rulers of south-western Iran and Iraq, and the Muslim caliphs who followed them. To them this was the 'eastern land' and included Jurjan, a province along the Caspian Sea, Kuhistan, the little-known region on the north-eastern edge of the Great Persian Desert, and the almost unsurveyed and now much impoverished Sistan (Sijistan) to the south. With one end almost in India and the other in the Caspian Sea, Khorasan was more than an extended buffer between traditional Iran and the world beyond the Oxus. It was one of the truly wealthy medieval provinces, and its wealth was summarized by its four best-known towns: Merv, at the edge of an oasis on the way to the Oxus; Nishapur, the Muslim capital known honorifically as *Iranshahr*, the City *par excellence* of Iran; Herat, on the way to the mountains of Afghanistan; and Balkh, the Mother of Cities, which, as we have seen, is equally part of Transoxiana. These were not, like Mediterranean cities, compact groupings of houses and monuments around and on top of each other; they were vast ensembles of administrative, religious, princely, mercantile, or living quarters recreated by successive generations or dynasties next to each other. Their ruins extend usually as far as the land or the availability of water permitted. This spread of the city makes for difficult archaeological surveys and it is no accident that so little is known about the physical history of these four cities, whose glory and wealth are described in the pages of all medieval geographers. Their function in history is, however, fairly clear in that they served as centres for the passage of goods and as military and administrative capitals. They provided for and profited from the urban world of merchants and artisans, and they protected the farmers who worked around the cities, in turn providing them with as many grown goods as the investment in irrigation by rulers and their delegates permitted.

As we move farther west, we may leave aside the towering mountain chain of the Elburz and the provinces of Mazanderan, Gilan, and Daylam, which encompass both snow-capped mountains and the sub-tropical Caspian shore. With some exceptions, this was an area whose importance appears to have been less in its monuments and civilization than in the fact that in its well protected valleys there flourished religious and political heterodoxies and that here were maintained ancient practices and ideas. It should be added, however, that these provinces are still very little known and that future studies and explorations may modify our present view. The more significant region from the point of view of the monuments is the area which actually skirted the central Iranian desert. First, the province of Kumis, with the cities of Bustam, Damghan, and Simnan, was mostly a narrow passageway. But near Rayy, in the neighbourhood of modern Tehran, the large Jibal province led from the desert to the high mountains of western Iran. With the province of Fars to the south, it was the heart-land of the very Iranian world which created the conception of the north-western frontier and the whole vision of Iran as centred around its 'national' dynasties: Achaemenids, Sasanians, and later the Safavids. The cities of Shiraz, Isfahan, Hamadan, Kashan, Qum, Qazvin, or Rayy were all at one time or another capitals of local dynasties or even of national dynasties. Except along a few of the major arteries which cut across the area — and which we have identified before — this was a region comparatively free of major invasions and perhaps less fully occupied than the north-eastern provinces with trade at the expense of agriculture, although the economic characteristics of Iranian provinces are rather difficult to determine clearly from reading medieval authors.

The next province, in all geographical logic, is Iraq, i.e., the southern part of the Mesopotamian valley. There a rich agriculture and a lively trade added to

29

the prestige of the imperial Abbasid capital, Baghdad. But while the intellectual and religious significance of the city of al-Mansur remained great until 1258, and while some major monuments were built there, not much is left of them. In fact, it could be shown that politically, artistically, and economically, Iraq's development had been the highest in early Islamic times and, in spite of several attempts to improve things, tended to decay in later centuries.

A province of considerable significance was the so-called Jazirah, a rather unwieldy area between the Tigris and Euphrates, now shared by the modern countries of Iraq, Turkey, and Syria. During the Middle Ages, in spite of constant efforts to make it agriculturally prosperous, the main function of the Jazirah was for commerce and transit. Along its rivers and between its mountains passed trade routes, invading armies, or bands of robbers, and its well-fortified cities — perched on mountain tops (fig. 396) or controlling strategic fords — often served as centres of operations for more or less respectable expeditions in search of booty. One of the main Jazirah routes, from Mosul to Diyarbakr, led on into Anatolia, while the other went to Aleppo and from there moved southward to Palestine and Syria. We will not concern ourselves much with this latter branch, but the northern road to Anatolia through the Jazirah met in central Anatolia another route which came directly from Iran through Azerbayjan and the Armenian Mountains.

It is on the central Anatolian plateau that our track ends. There a plateau with the large temperature variations of a continental mass is framed by high mountains plunging into the Mediterranean climate in the south and a luscious, almost sub-tropical world to the north. It has been said that the landscape of Anatolia, with its limited agricultural possibilities, its large pasture lands, its location near major trade routes connecting the Near East and the world beyond, and with its ancient commercial and military cities, is not unrelated to that of Central Asia, where we began our description of the lands whose monuments are here shown. The supposed physical similarity finds a parallel in the curious fact that both areas are now populated, for the most part, by Turkic peoples. It is largely during the time of the monuments illustrated in this book that the two areas became so populated, a fact which testifies to the importance of the historical changes which affected the whole of the Near East at that time. But the significance of the two extremities of the vast areas with which we are dealing can be particularly strongly emphasized by the fact that the first 230 and the last 200 of the photographs deal with their monuments.

SPACE AND TIME, PEOPLE AND PURPOSES

2. THE HISTORICAL SETTING:
UNTIL THE THIRTEENTH CENTURY

The definition of the physical setting in which our monuments are found can thus be made both on a level of generalization valid for the whole area and on a more detailed level, province by province. An understanding of the history which made these monuments possible can be reached from the points of view either of an œcumenical Islamic civilization or of the peculiar destinies of certain ethnic or regional entities. Since we will attempt to show that the monuments reflect both certain changes characteristic of the whole Near East and, as monuments of architecture, the possibilities inherent in locally available materials and the traditions of individual provinces, it will be useful to dwell simultaneously on the universal and local elements of Muslim culture and history during the centuries illustrated by the monuments.

In the late seventh and early eighth centuries the Muslim conquest stopped somewhat short of the Pyrenees and barely extended beyond the Oxus. Following a series of internecine wars between the Arab conquerors of the Near East, a many-faceted balance was established between the ancient traditions of the Orient — various Christian ones in Egypt, Syria, Spain, and parts of Mesopotamia, various Mazdean ones in western Iran, Soghd, Khorezm — and the new Arab faith, Islam, supported by an Arab military organization and by new Arab settlers or non-Arab converts in the old cities of the Near East as well as in a series of newly created cities. Until the early decades of the ninth century, this new synthesis was ruled either by Umayyad caliphs from Syria or by Abbasid caliphs from the new pan-Islamic capital of Baghdad; only Spain escaped, as early as 750, from the political control of the caliphal centres, with much in its culture remaining still closely tied with the Near East.

In the ninth century, there are signs from several directions that the synthesis elaborated earlier was crumbling. The unity of the faith was endangered by the mu'tazilite controversy on the nature of the revelation and by the progress made by the heterodox shi'ites who felt, among other things, that only descendants of the Prophet through his son-in-law Ali were entitled to the caliphate. The political unity of the empire was threatened by the *de facto*, if not *de jure*, independence of appointed governors in Tunisia, Egypt, and, most significantly for our purposes, Khorasan, where the rather remarkable dynasty of Arab governors known as the Tahirids succeeded in developing the prestige and wealth of the province in an aura of quasi-independent vice-royalty. The social balance between classes as well as between Muslims and non-Muslims or Arabs and non-Arabs began to lose its equilibrium, as the slave wars of the Zanj in the south of Iraq, originating in social injustice, weakened the very core of the empire, and as various revolts in Iraq and in the mountains of Iran showed the persistence of older Iranian religious movements. The caliphs could no longer rely on their Arab army and had to import Turkish slaves from Central Asia, thereby creating a mercenary army which did not usually succeed in integrating itself with the more traditional elements of early medieval Muslim society. Finally, on a semi-intellectual level, Arabs and Persians were trying to measure their respective ethnic characteristics and cultural contributions by debasing the characteristics and contributions of the other group.

During the course of the ninth century, the Abbasid caliphate usually managed to appear victorious over all these disruptive elements, but the struggle weakened the caliphate and the tenth century was, it is generally agreed, a sorry century for the descendants of Harun al-Rashid. Not only were Princes of the Faithful replaced, blinded, or even murdered by ambitious families of military commanders (the so-called *amirs al-umara*), but the unity of the faith was gone. The *de facto* rulers of Baghdad were shi'ites; first in North Africa and then, in 969, in Egypt a shi'ite counter-caliphate was established. Its newly founded capital, Cairo, would soon rival Baghdad in wealth, power, and learning; other shi'ite sects appeared in Yemen, Syria, and Iran. The 'universal' Muslim empire, in many ways an inheritance of the Hellenistic *koiné*, was broken and in its stead the separate 'provinces' began to grow and develop as political and cultural centres. The Buwayhid princes, who originated from the wild Persian provinces of Daylam, brutally controlled the caliphs in Baghdad and contributed only intermittently to the welfare of the capital. Their main contribution, however, was in developing western Iran, for it is in Rayy and Shiraz that they built gardens, palaces, rich libraries, enchanting pavilions, and lofty mausoleums for themselves and for their 'clients' (i.e., legal dependents or tribal associates). They patronized scholars and artists and reformed the agrarian and social structure of much of western Iran. The Hamdanids of the Jazirah and of northern Syria shared with the Buwayhids the responsibility for the weakening of the caliphate, but contributed also to the rebirth, economically and culturally, of Mosul, Aleppo, and of much of the middle Euphrates region.

While a number of minor dynasties — some of them not even converted to Islam — profited from the incoherence of the central caliphal authority to establish themselves in varying degrees of independence along the shores of the Caspian Sea, the most important changes took place all through the tenth century in Khorasan, Sistan, and Transoxiana. It is hardly possible to give a coherent chronology of the political developments of the century in a few sentences, since they overlap considerably. Two separate dynasties, however, that of the Saffarids (867–903 with several later revivals) of popular origin, centred in Sistan, and especially that of the Samanids (874–999), of aristocratic origin and centred in Bukhara and Samarkand, transformed north-eastern Iran from a military frontier into an area which could compete in wealth and sophistication with Baghdad and Cairo or Cordova. The peculiarity of this civilization was that, in keeping with contemporary moods, it was both universally Islamic and intensely local in its interests. It harboured and helped the celebrated philosopher Avicenna, the great physician al-Razi, and the mathematician and astronomer al-Biruni, all of whom were illustrious exponents of intellectual activities characteristic of the whole of Islam, and at the same time it was heavily involved in a tremendous revival of things Iranian. Not only were many translations from the Arabic or the Pahlevi accomplished there, but it was in north-eastern Iran also that medieval Persian poetry was created, as Rudaqi, born near Samarkand, began to write his odes, as Daqiqi began the Persian epic which the great Ferdosi was to complete in his immortal *Shahnameh*. The tenth century was not merely an intellectually brilliant moment in the history of Khorasan and Transoxiana. The wealth of the province was considerable; as the large land-owners settled in small castles surrounded by irrigated lands, the princes embellished the cities and developed the standard eastern Iranian urban type. Some aspects of its character can be gathered from the following excerpt from al-Narshakhi's *History of Bukhara:* 'the amir Sa'id Nasr ibn Ahmad ibn Isma'il al-Samani (301–331/913–943) ordered a court erected in the Rigistan. A very fine court was built which required much expense. Near the gate of his court he ordered a building erected for the officials so that each functionary had a separate bureau in his court. At the gate of the sultan's court were the bureau of the prime minister, the bureau of the treasurer, the bureau of the chief of the guards, the bureau of the postmaster, bureau of the chief of protocol, bureau of the private lands of the ruler, bureau of the chief of (the municipal) police, bureau of religious endowments, and bureau of the judges. He ordered the bureaus erected in such an arrangement. In the time of the amir Rashid 'Abd al-Malik ibn Nuh. . . his prime minister. . ., whose grave is in the quarter of the Mansur Gate in the vicinity of the Khan's bath house, built a wonderful mosque opposite the religious school. As a result (the beauty of) that place was enhanced by this mosque. . . .'(tr. R. N. Frye, Cambridge, 1954, pp. 25–6). In addition, superb palaces were set in the gardens which characterized the growing residential suburbs of the new urban centres.

But at the same time that this brilliant life of the mind and of the senses illuminated the great cities, there existed in the suburbs and in the country, especially along the frontier between settled lands and steppes, a wholly different world about which too little is known. On the basis of later events, however, it may be imagined as consisting of devoted Muslims organized in orders recalling those of Christian soldier-monks (*murabit*, living in *ribats*) and fighting both for the preservation of the Muslim world and for the conversion of non-Muslims. This world of the frontier fighter with its *ghazi* spirit existed elsewhere, on the Byzantine frontier and in North Africa, and thus is not peculiar to Transoxiana, except that in Transoxiana it had a particular impact on the events of the following century. Its presence illustrates once more that certain values peculiar to the whole of Islam were present in this most oriental outpost of the Muslim world.

Toward the end of the tenth century — a century so disastrous for the Muslim *oikoumené* and yet so brilliant for many of its provinces — an event of considerable importance took place in eastern Iran. For reasons that have not yet been fully explained, large-scale movements of Turkish tribes began to the north and north-east of the Samanid kingdom and the pressure on Islam increased, just as it increased on the Volga and the budding Russian principalities. One of the ways in which the Samanids met the pressure was to enrol some of the Turkish groups in their own army or to settle them on the frontier in order to defend the Samanids against other Turks. While interesting in conception, this plan ultimately failed, in that little by little the various provinces and sub-provinces of Transoxiana fell to Turkish tribes which, slowly but effectively, managed to transform into 'Turkestan' a so far predominantly Iranian area and also to transform into Turkey a part of Anatolia. These people became Muslims of a unique variety, combining the old *ghazi* spirit, a strong attachment to orthodoxy, and a fair number of more or less subdued pagan customs. They acquired a degree of Iranian culture; and they embarked on a fascinating series of conquests of their own, modifying considerably the Muslim world and extending its frontiers.

Since the vast majority of the monuments shown here were built during the two or three centuries which followed the appearance of the Turks in the service of the Samanids, and since it was indeed a crucial period in Islamic history, it is appropriate that we look at that history in some detail, trying always to balance the pan-Islamic and local significance of the characteristics to be described.

The chronological frame is easy to establish. The first dynasty to spring out of the Samanid fold was that of the Ghaznevids (962–1186), who established their capital in present Afghanistan, at Ghazni and Qal'ah-i Bust. They controlled Khorasan, but their main activity was in the conquest and control of much of northern India. Although significant for the history of Iran, the impact of the Ghaznevids on Iran and further western areas was not so great as the impact of the dynasty which emerged from the Ghaznevid army, that of the Seljuqs.

Seljuq was a chieftain whom the Qarakhanids had settled, with his tribe, on the marches of Central Asia. (The Qarakhanids were a small Turkish dynasty which ruled at the edge of the Samanid world.) Seljuq became a Muslim some time late in the tenth century. After numerous and highly confusing developments in the relations between Seljuq or his descendants and the various existing authorities, in the years 1035-40, two of Seljuq's grandsons, Tuhgril Beg and Chagri Beg, managed to wrest power from the Ghaznevids throughout most of Khorasan and to be recognized there by the commercial and other urban interests as their appropriate military protectors. At this juncture what might have been nothing more than a local episode acquired, so to speak, pan-Islamic features. For, as they successfully wrested Iranian cities from the Ghaznevids and also from other lesser rulers of sections of north-eastern Iran, the simple but shrewd princes and their followers realized — or were made to realize — the sad plight of the rightful Abbasid caliphate oppressed by heretical Buwayhid *amirs*.

It is of course difficult today to understand the exact prestige and power of the slogans of the past, and it is equally difficult to separate the effects of sheer expansionist strength from the rationalizations of expansion given after the fact; yet it does seem to be true that the title of 'client (i.e., associated with the family) of the Commander of the Faithful', which was assumed by Tughril, gave him a spiritual authority which increased as his physical strength grew. As has been shown by recent historical research, Tughril's power grew in two directions simultaneously as he assumed control over western Iran and his forces infiltrated Azerbayjan, Georgia, and Armenia along the northern route described above. The spiritual and institutional culmination of these activities occurred in 1055, when the Seljuq prince made his official entry into the caliphal capital of Baghdad. Having conquered Baghdad, he became the 'king of the East and of the West'; and jurists agreed that, as the *sultan*, he was possessed of a part of the oecumenical power reserved to caliphs alone. By then, of course, as the Seljuq prince and his immediate followers penetrated fully into the Establishment of the time and were accepted by it, the rift widened between them and those Turks who became the dreaded Turkomans of medieval chroniclers. They also were Turkish tribesmen but they were more interested in booty than in preserving the values of older Islam; furthermore, they were more affected by the rude simplicity of the *ghazi* faith (those at least who were converted to Islam) than by the intricacies of scholastic Islam. Thus, by the middle of the eleventh century, a Turkish prince brought up in the Turco-Iranian world of Transoxiana had become the official right arm of an Arab caliph who for over a century had been almost totally dependent on western Iranian princes. The main military force of the Near East consisted of Turkoman tribesmen, who, travelling in whole tribes, were both searching for places to settle and trying to widen Islam's frontiers.

For a whole century, with varying degrees of success, an almost direct succession of Seljuq princes — the so-called Great Seljuqs — were the primary force in the Near East. After 1071 Central Anatolia opened up to Turkoman tribes and to Seljuq princes. The continuing warfare between the Great Seljuqs and the heretical Fatimids of Egypt was considerably complicated by the intrusion of the Crusaders in 1099 and by the formation of the totally alien Latin Kingdom of Jerusalem. During this period the Seljuq centres were in western Iran and in Iraq. But as the decades of the twelfth century went by, the extreme ends of the Seljuq world began to wither away. In the north-east, in addition to minor nuisances such as the Qarluqs, the Qipchaqs, or even the Qara-Khitais — all Turkic dynasties of brief duration — there slowly grew the powerful house of the Khorezm-shahs, which managed to control most of Khorasan, even though constantly threatened by revolts, intrigues, and invasions from farther north and east. In southern Iran and in Anatolia, local branches of the main Seljuq stem flourished, and in Anatolia in particular they managed to remain quite strong and independent through complex systems of alliances with their Christian neighbours. In Azerbayjan local Shirvan Shahs maintained a quasi-independence from the central authority. It is in Iraq, the Jazirah, and Syria that, largely as a result of the Crusades, the most considerable changes took place in the twelfth century. As a response to the Frankish challenge, a complex hierarchy of Turkish and Kurdish princes established itself. Every town and village was transformed into a fortress for some feudal baron. These rulers developed a complex system of allegiances to each other and thus, although they were independent, their destinies were interlocked. One of the main results of this powerful growth of a rejuvenated Islam in Syria was that in 1171 Egypt was taken away from the Fatimids and restored to orthodoxy.

This complicated state of affairs, in which the immense stretch of the Islamic world from the Mediterranean to India and Siberia was governed in small units with Turks and Kurds forming the preponderant military force, lasted until the second decade of the thirteenth century. Between 1218, when the ruling Khorezm-shah of the time, Muhammad, executed a group of Mongol envoys of Chinghiz Khan, and 1307–8, when the last Seljuq prince of Anatolia gave way to a Mongol governor, the Mongol invasion completely destroyed the world created by the Great Seljuqs in the middle of the eleventh century. This destruction was not an instantaneous one, and the effects of the Mongol invasion varied considerably from one province to the other. Transoxiana and Khorasan were left in ruins, and cities like Balkh and Nishapur disappeared. In central Persia, the ancient city of Rayy was abandoned, while numerous other cities were sacked, but the damage was not as permanent as in the east. Baghdad was sacked in 1258 and the last Abbasid caliph was killed, but, thanks to the diplomacy of Badr al-din Lu'lu', Mosul was spared, at least for a while. Northern and central Syria surrendered to the Mongol onslaught until the Mamluk army from Egypt succeeded in checking it at the battle of Ayn Jalut in 1260. The Seljuqs of Anatolia did not suffer directly from the Mongols, who contented themselves with an overlordship of the Anatolian provinces, but various internal difficulties led to their demise in the first decade of the fourteenth century and to their replacement by a plethora of small Turkish states, out of which the Ottoman eventually emerged as the most powerful.

Such is the chronological framework. It begins with the massive movement into the traditional Muslim world of Turks from Central Asia, who managed to restore something of the former grandeur and unity of the orthodox Muslim world; and it ends with the destructive Mongol invasion which issued from the same Central Asia and which, directly or indirectly, affected all parts of the Near East during most of the thirteenth century. Out of our rapid survey of the main political events, three features may be singled out as characterizing the political dynamism of the period: the ubiquitousness of the Turks — and to a more limited degree of the Kurds — i.e., of nomadic or mountain peoples who until then had lived on the fringes of high Muslim culture and whose presence we have defined as a characteristic of the human geography of the Near East; the apparently constant movement of people from east to west, to which the Crusaders were but a foreign and artificial exception; and the multiplicity of centres in which more or less independent princelings established themselves as pseudo-feudal lords.

3. THE SOCIAL AND CULTURAL SETTING: ELEVENTH TO THIRTEENTH CENTURIES

To these characteristics must be added others which serve to explain more fully the character and the purposes of the monuments. The first of these characteristics lies in the social structure of the world of the eleventh through thirteenth centuries. On this point our information is still remarkably insufficient, but the indications provided by archaeological documents suggest that, even though considerable regional variations must have existed, the centres of social and political or cultural life were the cities, and that there were in each urban centre separate levels of social organization and consciousness, each of which was fully related to its counterpart in other cities as it was connected with the other social levels within its own city — perhaps even more so. Of these levels we may identify four as having had an ascertainable relationship to the monuments of the time. It must, however, be emphasized that the conclusions to be presented here are based less on literary sources than on the evidence suggested by the monuments themselves, both in architecture and the other arts; their full justification must await the publication of detailed monographs and, since some, at least, of the conclusions may eventually have to be modified, it would be more appropriate to consider them as working hypotheses.

The first identifiable level comprises the military aristocracy, the Turkish or Kurdish princes — among whom personages of other ethnic origins appear occasionally, such as the Armenian Badr al-din Lu'lu' — who occupied the newly built or rebuilt citadels (figs. 519–20), who reconstructed the walls of the cities, and who often enough in the Jazirah, Syria, and Anatolia, revived into major centres places which had lost all significance centuries earlier. They even created new centres, such as Dunaysir (figs. 514–15) which controlled a major east-west route on the northern edge of the Syrian desert. At their simplest level these military leaders, with their tribal or mercenary armies, were but robber barons such as were known in medieval Europe as well. But the interesting phenomenon of the period is that this social class adopted, in many instances, ideas and ideals of a more traditionally Islamic or even pre-Islamic character, giving them a historical significance greater than that of the average military band. On the highest level, that of the Great Seljuqs in Iran and in western Iran or that of a Saladin fighting the Crusades, the identification with the Muslim tradition was almost complete. In the case of Saladin it was a comparatively simple matter, since he was so obviously defending the orthodox faith against hetero-

doxy and against infidels. In the case of the Great Seljuqs, the identification was
not merely with a religious Islamic tradition — although we shall see that that
was also so — but also with a synthesis of pre-Islamic, especially Iranian, ideas
with new Muslim ones. The point appears clearly in the *Siasset-nameh*, the book
of political conduct written by Nizam al Mulk, the celebrated vizier (d. 1092) of
the Seljuq prince Malik-shah: 'For it was ordained by the All-Highest,' wrote
Nizam al-Mulk, 'that at this time the history of past eras be recreated and that
it follow the example of the deeds of past kings and that men be granted an
unheard-of happiness. To this effect He brought out the ruler of the world, the
great sultan issued from two great roots [i.e., presumably Iranian and Turanian
through the descendants of Afrasiyab and Siyavush], since rule and leadership
belonged to these families from father to son as far back as the time of Afrasiyab.'
The Seljuq prince here appears not merely as the sultan and right hand of the
caliph, but as the heir to a whole tradition of Iranian kingship, which at this
very time was being written up and popularized not only in the *Shah-nameh*,
but in a whole series of similar epics emphasizing other aspects of the Iranian
legend. It appears, then, that at least one facet of the Turkish princes' historical
function was that, through Iranian legists and intellectuals, they embodied,
perpetuated, and carried through the Near East themes of Iranian regal traditions. Thus it is that, in Anatolia in particular, Seljuq princes bore names of
Turkish (Qilij Arslan), Iranian (Key-Khosrow), or Arabic Islamic ('Izz al-din,
Sulayman) origins.

If from the level of the Great Seljuqs, one moves down to smaller princes,
it becomes, of course, much more difficult to assess their characteristics, since
our documentation is often limited. On the Turkish princes of north-eastern
Iran, even on the Ghaznevids, our lack of sufficient information or of adequate
studies is all the more unfortunate since the influences of these princes, of their
lives and mores, on subsequent dynasties can clearly be established. Mahmud
of Ghaznah's patronage of Ferdosi, even though not entirely appreciated by the
poet, is at least an indication of the prince's Iranian interests. In Anatolia and
in the Jazirah, two sets of available sources suggest a more complex explanation
of the princes' mentality. The first source consists of chronicles, such as the
recently translated chronicle of the Seljuqs of Anatolia written by Ibn Bibi.
The other source is archaeological documents, in particular coins and the illustrations of the 'Book that combines Theory and Practice useful in the craft
of Ingenious Contrivances' (known for short as the *Automata*) of al-Jazari, composed in the late twelfth and very early thirteenth centuries for an Ortoqid
prince who ruled at Hisn Kayfa, on the upper Tigris.

From Ibn Bibi's chronicle, we may learn of the marriage of 'Izz al-din Kay-ka'us to the daughter of some other prince, for it was a social affair of considerable significance in which money and riches were thrown to the throngs in a manner curiously reminiscent of one of the most celebrated marriages of early Abbasid times, the marriage of al-Ma'mun to Buran. In fact, it may be suggested that the early marriage served as a model for the one in Konya. The coins of the Anatolian Seljuq princes and of the Ortoqids are remarkable for the consistency with which they show imagery of pre-Islamic origin, such as the heads of Roman and Byzantine emperors who had ruled in Anatolia, in co-existence with more understandable Turkish or Iranian symbols. The book of *Automata* illustrates all sorts of machines made for princes. The technical aspects of the contrivances doubtlessly derived from Greek models, as has been shown more than once, but the final object, in a number of major instances, clearly reflected ideals of princely life of Abbasid and Fatimid origins — such as boating parties or elaborate clocks — or symbols of the Abbasid imperial tradition, such as a celebrated representation of the original Baghdad palace with its two domes and its rider on top of the whole building. What these instances from the lives of the princes or of the things made for them show is that these minor rulers scattered in the cities of Syria, the Jazirah, or Anatolia represented more than an influx of Turkish military men and more than the impact of Iranian names or ideas; for around them congregated ideals belonging more strictly to an Islamic imperial tradition as it had been created during the first centuries of the new faith. At times even local aspirations and aims appeared among the elements which dictated the policies of the princes or which inspired their way of life. These ideals, inspirations, and aims were not usually thought of by the princes themselves, nor were they commonly attempts on their part to espouse as their own the ideas and purposes of the cities whose rulers they became. It is rather that, in order to maintain their realms as functioning units, the princes had to surround themselves with a court or at least a retinue of 'people of the sword' (officers and gendarmes of all kinds) and of 'people of the pen' (viziers, tax collectors, scribes, and so forth). The latter were usually more learned than their masters and it is through them, in all likelihood, that various ideals of the past were carried on to the new princes.

It is obvious enough that the position and wealth of the princes made them the prime patrons of monuments. They were responsible for fortresses, city walls, palaces, and hippodromes; they also sponsored or repaired religious institutions, such as mosques and schools; they perpetuated their own names through tombs and showed their piety by endowing hospitals, fountains, and other such philanthropic organizations. And it is for them that were made many of the objects, especially in metalwork, which depicted various aspects of their lives. In a curious way they also appeared as guarantors of the value of works of art which they could not in any way appreciate; thus it is that many works of Arabic literature acquired frontispieces with more or less standardized representations of ruling princes, for, even though most of them were hardly likely to understand and appreciate the literature, their images or symbols served to give prestige to the book.

Besides the princes there existed a second level of society which also sponsored the construction of buildings and the manufacture of objects. It was the level of the urban bourgeoisie, composed of merchants and of artisans. As early as in the tenth century, as the central authority of the caliphs began to decline, in many towns representative citizens organized themselves to protect their interests and to defend their cities. The occupations of these citizens, as well as the extent of their wealth or culture, obviously varied from place to place, but in most instances they were not so much manufacturers as tradesmen, the very tradesmen whose initiative and organization led Muslims as far east as China. As the military aristocracy took power in the eleventh century, much of the political and military importance of these urban groups was given up to the Turks and Kurds, but their social and cultural prestige remained unimpaired. In eastern Iran most of the earliest objects of brass and bronze, with the characteristic silver inlay technique, which was to have such tremendous development in the late twelfth and the thirteenth century, were made for merchants and artisans, some of whom had acquired titles usually reserved for military men. It is to this urban milieu that we owe one of the most extraordinary documents of the thirteenth century, a cycle of illustrations of the best-seller of the time, al-Hariri's *Maqamat*, in which the life of the Arab bourgeoisie, at work or at rest, is shown in most of its aspects with an extraordinary precision and often with a strange sense of humour. Another way in which the importance of this group can be seen is more apparent in Syria than elsewhere in the Islamic world. It is a curious fact that in Damascus, for instance, out of the dozens of twelfth and thirteenth century buildings which have survived, very few within the walls of the older city are of large size and only suburban constructions achieved some magnitude. The reason probably is that land in cities was expensive, because it was owned by locally entrenched families who were powerful enough to prevent their land from being expropriated for large new building programmes. The signs indicating the importance of this urban group vary from region to region and their significance as patrons of architecture was not so great as that of the princes, but their direct or indirect influence can be felt throughout this time.

A third category of people with an identifiable impact on architecture is not, properly speaking, a social class, since its impact was felt at many different levels, and its influence appears not so much in individual sponsorship of architecture but as a spiritual force behind the patrons. This group consisted of what already at this time one might call the religious institution. Islam, as everyone knows, did not have an ecclesiastical structure comparable to that of Christianity. Nevertheless, certain developments of the faith from the eleventh century on created a body of men whose main concern was to take care of the intellectual and spiritual needs of the faithful, although, with the exceptions of certain sects and a few mystical orders, there never developed a hierarchically organized body of men with a definable independence from secular power.

Two such developments are of particular significance. The first one is symbolized by the institution of the *madrasah*. Its origins lie in the tremendous progress made by heterodox movements in the ninth and tenth centuries. In order to fight these, the Great Seljuqs engaged in a systematic effort to re-educate the Muslim masses in the ways of orthodoxy; but it was no longer quite the old orthodoxy. Rather, it appeared first as a new synthesis of religious, philosophical, and legal principles known as *a'sharism*, and then as variants thereof or even counterparts to it, developed within the framework of the main schools of law. The programme of re-education was effected through *madrasahs* (lit., " school "), and from eastern Iran to Egypt and Anatolia *madrasahs* were endowed by ruling princes or pious men of diverse social backgrounds in order to teach and expound various brands of orthodoxy. The most celebrated early *madrasahs* were those built in the late eleventh century by the great vizier Nizam al-Mulk and it is particularly unfortunate that none of these has remained, so that we cannot even guess at their physical arrangements. The example of Nizam al-Mulk was soon followed by others, and the building of *madrasahs* became the single most common way in which the wealthy could show their worldly successes, preserve their wealth by making their endowment inalienable, and prove their piety and concern for the spiritual welfare of others. To each of these *madrasahs* were attached teachers as well as librarians, copyists, fellowship students, and other scholars, making up a body of men who wielded considerable power in the social and spiritual life of the city.

But there is yet another level at which the faith made itself felt as an inspiration for monumental constructions. While the learned world of the *madrasahs* indulged in often abstruse intellectual and legal constructions, a more popular development of Islam was the growth of mystical and activist movements. We have already mentioned the purely activist ones as they existed on the frontiers of Islam and as they were embodied in the *ghazi* spirit. In the twelfth century — and perhaps even earlier — such movements appeared in the cities of the interior as is evidenced by the fact that *ribats* are mentioned by most city chroniclers. It has not, however, been clearly established as yet what the exact functions of these institutions were outside of the frontier areas. As to mysticism, known in Islam under the generic term of sufism, it did not consist merely of individuals with varying spiritual experiences and doctrines but soon involved orders of brotherhood which permeated all social levels and developed into one of the liveliest elements in the social and spiritual make-up of the Muslim world. The establishment in which followers of one or the other of the many more or less extensive orders lived was the *khangah*, which became both a permanent dwelling place for those who devoted their lives to spiritual guidance or to meditation and a place to which individuals could come for temporary retreats. The impact of the sufis did not, however, come merely from the fact that they persuaded wealthy people or princes to sponsor their monasteries. They also introduced and developed within Islam a note of private worship, as opposed to the community worship characteristic of earlier times, and the cult of individual holy men as the source of holiness for others. Both of these features had a considerable effect on monuments of architecture, even when those monuments were not directly sponsored by mystics or mystic orders. Sufi emphasis on the individual explains the growth of mausoleums and of a whole paraphernalia of supporting institutions such as guest houses, pilgrimages, kitchens for the poor; but it also contributed to the replacement of the huge congregational mosques of the first centuries of Islam with a multitude of small sanctuaries which stressed private devotions in a quiet setting conducive to prayer and meditation.

Other social groups could be identified who had, no doubt, an impact on the architecture, but our information is usually so scanty that the impact becomes difficult to evaluate. For instance, there are the artisans and architects, whose names we often know (especially in Anatolia and Azerbayjan) but whose precise impact on the monument has not yet been fully determined. There are also the non-Muslims. Their architecture is not represented in this album, but it should be noted that especially the heterodox Christian communities, Armenians, Jacobites, and Nestorians, were quite active within the framework of the Muslim empire. This had, of course, always been so, but during this period of consider-

43

able change and movement throughout the Near East, Christian involvement in economic and political affairs was considerable, especially in Anatolia, the Jazirah, and certain parts of Iran, even though these Christian communities suffered at times from the impact of the Crusades. Not as brilliant as the Muslims in their remaining architectural creations — although a number of churches of the thirteenth century in the area of Mosul and in the mountains of south-eastern Turkey are quite interesting — the Christians and the Jews formed an integral part of most of the cities in which the monuments illustrated in this volume are found. And many of the changes in styles or mood attributable to this period can be understood only if these non-Muslim groups are kept in mind.

If, then, one tries to summarize the essential features of the eleventh through thirteenth centuries in the vast area which we have defined earlier and in which a closely connected sequence of events took place, the first question that poses itself is whether a name could be given to this period. It has been called the Seljuq period on the correct grounds that the specific tribe of Turks known as the Seljuqs was most strongly involved in its formative decades. Yet we have seen that the Seljuqs did not create the new order of things, but were, rather, its carriers and its catalysts, and that many others besides the Turks participated in the richly creative period. Perhaps a more appropriate name for this period would be 'the second Islamic classicism', the first one being the time in the eighth and ninth centuries when, under the early Abbasids and the Umayyads of Syria and of Spain, a peculiarly Islamic synthesis took place between the ancient Mediterranean and western Asiatic cultures and the new faith and state. In our period a new series of syntheses took place. Out of the social and religious crises of the tenth century a new order was established with a revived orthodoxy and a powerful sufism as well as with an extensive development of urban centres. New people — Turks, Kurds, various Christian groups of Anatolia, Hindus of India — became incorporated into the Muslim world, whether or not they immediately adopted the Muslim faith. In spite of a political fragmentation of authority, both in theory, through the complex system of allegiances which led up to a spiritually revivified caliphate and to a fairly strong sultanate, and in practice, through an intensity of commercial and intellectual contacts, a certain unity existed in the vast entity which stretched from the Nile and the gates of Constantinople to the Indus Plain and the Altai Mountains. It was also a time when Iran, conquered as early as the seventh century, truly asserted itself as the most lively component of the Islamic *oikoumené*. To be sure, Arabic was still the major linguistic vehicle throughout, and its preponderance was almost total in the religious sphere. Yet the significant point about this time is not only that it was a brilliant period of Persian literature and art, but that the Persian literature of the time was greater than the Arabic; that it was Persians for the most part who served as intellectual and political advisers for the Turkish princes; and that so many themes and ideas of art and architecture were carried from east to west. This is not to deny the originality of solutions to architectural problems or of artistic expressions in painting and in the decorative arts which were found in Syria, Egypt, or the partly Iranized Iraq; it is rather that these achievements were not quite so remarkable as those of Iran. That this was so stemmed partly from the fact that the first Islamic classicism, by being so closely tied to the Arab world in which it had developed, tended to restrict the ideal toward which art and thought were striving in this second period of Islamic classicism.

One further observation emerges from our brief presentation, and it is all the more important to emphasize it since the remaining monuments reveal it very imperfectly. It is the immense diversification of the purposes of monumental architecture. Much of what remains consists of religious buildings, but these no longer are, as in earlier periods, large mosques for whole congregations. Instead congregational mosques, often small ones, are found alongside schools, private sanctuaries, tombs, monasteries. As the religious institution developed, so did its monuments. In addition, the complex society of the time also sponsored secular buildings. Fortresses, caravanseraglios, city walls, palaces, houses, hospitals, and gardens were built in considerable numbers and, from the pitifully few that are still standing and from inadequate early descriptions, it is rather difficult to imagine what they must have been. Yet often, since religious architecture tends always to the traditional, it was the monuments of secular architecture that created new tastes, and embodied new ideas. The existence of such a secular architecture must be recalled in any attempt to explain the architecture of the time. It should be added also that the variety of purposes for architectural constructions, which developed at this time, was to remain during the centuries to come. In this sense the second classical period of Islam developed needs and purposes to be served by monumental architecture which, with a number of exceptions, inspired most Islamic buildings almost until the nineteenth century.

The importance of this period rests not only in the fact that it is the time when so many of the ethnic, literary, religious, social, and artistic features of traditional Islam were created. It is also significant that the period is more or less contemporary with Romanesque and early Gothic Europe — i.e., with the very time when the most sumptuous Western medieval art was created. The possible correlations between the two phenomena are not necessarily relations of cause and effect, as has been believed by some. There is, it is true, little doubt that in secular art and in certain decorative themes the Islamic world did influence those parts of western Christendom — Italy, Spain, southern France — which were closest to it. But, more importantly, the swell of energies and the intensity of creative effort, in art as well as in the social and political institutions which characterized the Near East at this time, existed also in the West. The historical tragedy of the Near East was that the destructions of the Mongol conquest sapped some of this energy and left a Near Eastern world whose pace and growth had considerably slackened.

4. THE LATER PERIODS

After the traumatic invasion, the Islamic world of the Near East resettled itself into four sharply separated areas which still today divide the Near East: an Arab world comprising Egypt and most of the Fertile Crescent, a Turkish world in Anatolia and the northern Jazirah, a purely Iranian world extending from the Zagros mountains through Khorasan, and an ethnically Turkified but still, culturally, partly Iranian world in Azerbayjan and Transoxiana. The Arab world of the Mamluks in Egypt and Syria was the only one of the four which clearly continued, in the second half of the thirteenth century, patterns of culture and society similar to those of the preceding period; and the great Mamluk monuments of Cairo, Jerusalem, and Aleppo (figs. 515 ff.) still remain to testify to the superb technical qualities of the builders of the late thirteenth, fourteenth, and fifteenth centuries. They are, however, particularly well known and have often been studied.

The monuments which followed the Mongol conquest are comparatively less well known in Anatolia and in Iran, where they have been overshadowed by the supreme achievements of Ottoman architecture from about 1400 onward and by those of the Safavids after 1500. Most of Anatolia was then divided between a sizeable and variable number of principalities (*beyliks*) which fought with each other not so much for supremacy as for survival, either as tribal entities or as controlling powers over certain routes and certain coastal areas. Much is still unknown about the religious, social, and intellectual ferments that took place in these principalities and among the Turks or converts of Anatolia, and which paved the way for the eventual formation of the Ottoman empire.

The history and culture of Iran during the fourteenth and fifteenth centuries is far more complex. For the sake of clarity, it may be divided into three separate parts, even though some of the developments to be discussed separately took place concurrently. First, until the forties of the fourteenth century, the major power was in the hands of the Mongol house of the Ilkhans. Their centre was in north-western Iran, with Tabriz and Sultaniyah as the main cities. Various reforms re-established the economy of the area, and to the eyes of travellers from east and west the Ilkhanid empire was a brilliant and powerful one, in which a major cultural synthesis was created using themes and men from as far as Western Europe or China. With the Mongols ruling, the population of Azerbayjan was becoming fully Turkified, while the administration, except for the army, was mostly in the hands of Persians. A second development characterized the middle of the century, when the power of the Ilkhanid dynasty weakened, and authority was held in separate parts of western and southern Iran by smaller dynasties, some Iranian, others Turkish, some even Mongol. It is during these first two periods that the first major schools of Persian miniature painting can be identified.

The third period witnesses a complete shift of the centre of gravity from the west to the east. The main cause for the shift was Tamerlane, the great Mongol prince born in 1335. It is in 1380 that he embarked on a series of campaigns in the Near East which, by the time of his death in 1405, made him the greatest conqueror the world has ever known. He established his capital in Samarkand, which he embellished and built up in a manner which struck the Spanish envoy, Clavijo, so forcefully that he left us a memorable description of the feverish building activity he saw there: alongside rows of superb tents in gardens, a world of wealthy nomads perpetuated their names through the construction of *madrasahs*, tombs, and mosques. Through almost the end of the fifteenth century Timurid princes controlled north-eastern Iran, even though they often had to battle against rebellious vassals or new dynasties such as that of the Uzbeks, who managed to establish themselves in Bukhara and Samarkand around 1500, at the very time that the Safavids became masters of the rest of Iran. The Timurids escaped into India where their dynasty was still destined to have a great history. As the Safavids rose to their great glory in western Iran, Central Asia receded somewhat from the consciousness of the Near East and from the rest of the world. It is one of the merits of this collection of photographs that it has made accessible photographs of monuments built as late as the seventeenth century by the Uzbek rulers of Central Asia, monuments which so far have been known almost exclusively in Russian publications.

The social and intellectual characteristics of Iran and Central Asia during the two or three centuries which followed the Mongol conquest are both more and less difficult to define than those of the preceding period. The purposes and functions of the buildings tended to be the ones developed before the Mongol conquest. Most of the energy observed in the earlier period appeared now only in the courts of the main rulers. They became the sole patrons of architecture and it is around them that artists of all kinds were gathered. What was thereby gained in quality of execution may at times have been achieved at the expense of originality of composition and vitality. The great and superb *madrasahs*, monasteries, tombs, and palaces of these centuries (an exception should probably be made for the monuments of Mashhad) were more often than not expressions of royal glory alone and hardly in harmony with the more profound social and spiritual needs of the population, as had so often been the case in the preceding centuries.

II. THE MONUMENTS

The purpose of this chapter is to identify the monuments which are illustrated. The identifications are made by city and in the approximate order in which the photographs appear. Since so few Islamic monuments have ever been adequately published and since for many of them we do not even possess an adequate plan, it has not always been possible to give more than minimal information on the character of the monuments and on their history. A more extensive commentary has been made for such buildings — for instance in Russian Central Asia — as are less easily accessible than others or for which an adequate bibliography exists only in less common languages. References to written works other than the ones mentioned in the bibliographical notes at the end of the volume have been limited either to particularly important studies or to such studies as make a central point for the identification of the monuments.

Two other preliminary remarks should be made. First, many monuments, especially in Iran, were built over many centuries; the dates mentioned in the commentary usually refer to the parts of the buildings which are actually illustrated and should not always be construed as dating the whole building. The warning is all the more important since there are so few Iranian buildings for which we have any kind of full archaeological history. Second, numerous though the buildings are which have been here illustrated, they cannot of course represent the sum total of the architectural production of the eleventh

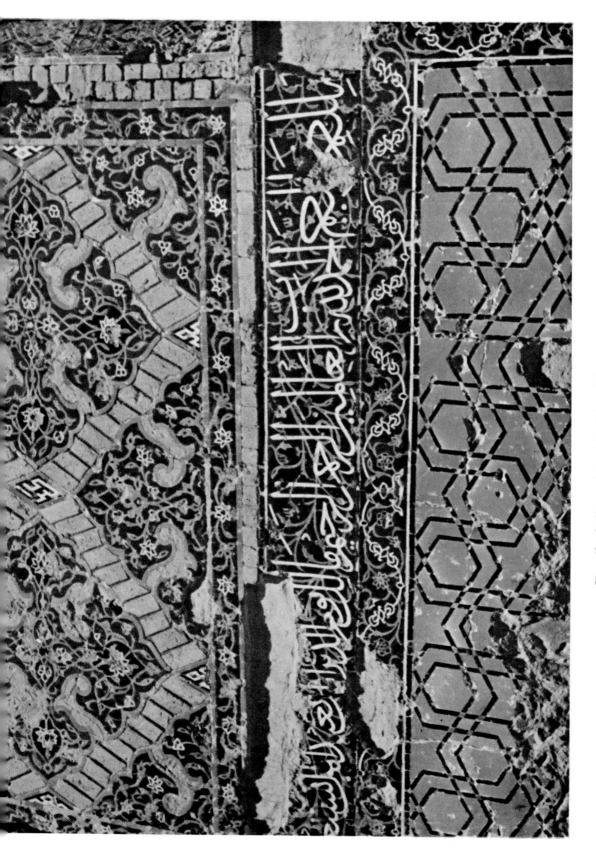

Detail of tilework in the Blue Mosque of Tabriz

through fifteenth centuries. Certain regions, such as northern Azerbayjan, are difficult to visit and some crucial buildings may have been underplayed, or not have been studied enough to allow for a strict dating of their decoration. In as celebrated a monument as the great mosque at Isfahan, it is still uncertain which parts of the decoration belong to what period and to what degree they were redone over the centuries. It is to be hoped that this presentation may lead to an eventual re-examination of most of these monuments. Finally it should be added that, since the writer has not visited all the places illustrated, and has not read all the accounts of buildings extending from Siberia almost to Constantinople, it is likely that a number of factual errors, including errors of identification, have occurred. It is only hoped that they are not so numerous as to make the following identifications less useful.

Bukhara

The Tomb of the Samanids (figs. 1 and 2): this celebrated monument has been called the mausoleum of Ismail the Samanid. Recent discoveries have shown this attribution to be incorrect. The building was probably a collective mausoleum for several princes of the dynasty and can be dated some time between 913 and 943. It is the fourth earliest known Islamic mausoleum. Neither its shape — a perfect 'canopy' mausoleum symmetrical on four axes with four small decorative domes framing the large central one on the outside only — nor its extraordinary and unique use of brickwork have yet been satisfactorily explained; cf. L. Rempel in *Bull. Amer. Inst. for Persian Art and Archaeology*, vol. IV (1935) and O. Grabar, 'The Earliest Islamic Mausoleums' (*Ars Orientalis* VI) (forthcoming).

The mosque Maghak-i Attari (figs. 3–8) (mosque of the pit of the druggists) has been very much restored over the centuries. It is a small building and was probably a private hall of prayers built by and for a precise neighbourhood. It may have been the mosque Maghak referred to in a medieval History of Bukhara (al-Narshakhi, *The History of Bukhara*, tr. R. N. Frye, Cambridge, 1954, p. 64), since traces have been discovered of tenth-century columns inside the building. But its most remarkable feature is an asymmetrically set southern façade which has been dated in the early part of the twelfth century by the latest and most authoritative study of the subject (V. A. Nilsen, *Monumentalnaia Arhitektura Buharskogo Oazisa*, Tashkent, 1956, pp. 70 ff.). The façade has been very much damaged but contains several noteworthy features: the use of rounded pilasters as in the celebrated Rabat-i Malik in the desert between

D

Bukhara and Samarkand, and a combination of brick work, stucco, and alabaster for the creation of one type of decorative effect, while another type is created simply with geometrically arranged bricks and stucco.

Most of the so-called Kalayan mosque was built in 1514 over an older and so far undatable building. But the remarkable minaret (45·6 metres high) belongs to an earlier construction (figs. 10–12), which can be identified as that of the Qarakhanid Arslan shah; it is datable in 1127 by an inscription with the prince's name and a reference in al-Narshakhi (p. 51; cf. Nilsen, pp. 83 ff.). The building is remarkable for the decorative use made of the brick arranged in concentric rings of various designs. This type of design was to spread from Central Asia all the way to Mesopotamia and Syria. According to the study of the monument made by Nilsen, the upper part of the minaret is contemporary with the main part of the cylinder, in spite of common assertions to the contrary.

The Namazgah mosque (fig. 14), in its present shape, is a sixteenth century building, but parts of its interior are as early as the twelfth and it may have been the main part of a *musalla* or prayer hall for special occasions, outside the walls of the city.

The minaret in Vabkent (fig. 13) is dated by an inscription in 595 A.H./A.D. 1198–9. It was built by the *sadr* Burhan al-Din Abd al-Aziz II, of the dynasty of religious leaders who ruled Bukhara during parts of the twelfth century. Although a little smaller and decoratively less spectacular, it is closely related to the Kalayan minaret, of which it is supposed to be an imitation (Nilsen, pp. 91 ff.).

The mausoleum of Buyan-Quly-khan (fig. 30) is the earliest remaining construction in Bukhara after the Mongol cataclysm. The personage for whom it was built was killed in 1358 and the building should be dated around that time. Many ornamental details and techniques relate this mausoleum to the pre-Mongol period, but, in spite of their complexity, the designs have been frozen and become more obvious than in the past. It is the first building in the city to use a polychrome decoration.

The *Mir-i Arab madrasah* (figs. 15–16) was built between 1530 and 1536 by the *shaykh* of an order of dervishes, the Yemenite Abdallah. Its peculiarity lies in the fact that the corners of the building were used as burial places for holy men and for the *khan* of Bukhara, Ubaydallah. A complete description is found in the study by L. Rempel and G. A. Pugachenkova listed in the bibliography.

The two *madrasahs* of Ulugh beg (figs. 17–18) and of Abd al-Azia khan (figs. 19–20), facing each other, form a superb ensemble. The first one was built in 1417 and considerably restored in 1586, with some of the faience work as late as the seventeenth century. The second one is dated in 1652 and represents the last great moments in Central Asia of the Timurid architectural tradition (Pugachenkova-Rempel, pp. 76 ff.).

A similar ensemble is created by the *madrasahs* of Abd Allah khan (second half of the sixteenth century) (figs. 21–3) and of Madar-i Shah (same period, fig. 24); the two buildings face each other and illustrate other variations of the Timurid tradition.

The *khangah* of Nadir Divan-beg (fig. 29) was actually part of a composite building which comprised a *madrasah* as well as a monastery for holy men. It was built in the first half of the seventeenth century and is remarkable for the consistency with which themes of decoration and systems of proportion created almost four centuries earlier were still kept up.

Some five kilometres from the town is found the large architectural complex known as the *Char Bakr* (figs. 25–8). Basically it was a necropolis such as those known from Samarkand, Cairo, and a number of other cities in the Near East. Around the burials holy places developed and with them official buildings, such as the mosque illustrated here, which was built for the most part around 1560–3. Its major peculiarity is that it had a court surrounded by buildings on three sides only, a type of composition which seems to be more closely related to the architectural type of the *musalla* (lit., 'place for prayer', usually outside the city and used only on certain days of major festivals) than to the traditional congregational type of mosque. Here again, however, Timurid models exist for the Char Bakr example, such as the mausoleum of Jamal al-Haqq wa al-Din in Anau (now destroyed by earthquake).

Samarkand

The monument known as the *Gur-i Amir* is the best known of the architectural treasures of Samarkand, because of its association with the tomb of Tamerlane (figs. 31–8). The history of the building is in fact much more complex than has usually been assumed. It was meant to be the monumental tomb in the midst of a *madrasah* and *khangah* complex which Tamerlane ordered in commemoration of his favourite nephew, Muhammad Sultan, who died in 1403. Tamerlane supervised the work until his own death in 1405. At this time the mausoleum became a sort of family shrine in which most of the major princes of the dynasty were buried. As a result it was added to and worked on until the middle of the fifteenth century. Aside from its unusual plan, which combined the characteristics of early mausoleums with a mosque-like façade, the building is famous for its superb ribbed dome on a high drum, for the excellence of the coloured tiles which cover most of its wall surfaces, and for the quality of the designs used on other materials, such as wood or marble (fig. 34), which were so prominently employed in the construction. As a family shrine it received all the care the dynasty could afford. Thus may be explained the fact that one of the masters who worked there came all the way from Isfahan (Pugachenkova-Rempel, pp. 119 ff.).

The mosque of *Bibi Khanum* (figs. 39–58) shares with the Timurid mausoleum the first position among the monuments of Samarkand. Although legend has associated Timur's consort with the construction of the building, it has now been shown (basic study by Sh. E. Ratiia, *Mechet Bibi-Hanym v Samarkande* Moscow, 1950) that the so-called mosque of Bibi Khanum was in fact the congregational mosque ordered by Tamerlane to replace an older building. It was begun on May 11, 1399, at an astrologically favourable moment, and workers from all over the Timurid world were called to participate in a construction which has the additional unique feature of having been illustrated in a manuscript of the late fifteenth century. Although based on a plan created several centuries earlier of a court with four large *eyvans* (i.e., rectangular vaulted halls closed on three sides and opening to the outside on the fourth) one of which is also the main entrance, the mosque of Samarkand introduces several novel features. First, its superb, and now much ruined, portal occupied an extraordinary position on the façade of the building; by its shape it announces at the entrance of the building the holy hall of prayers which is on the same axis on the other side of the inner court. A second remarkable feature of the building is its use of domes and minarets. Neither feature is new as such, but the use of domes behind every *eyvan* and over the whole area between *eyvans* where some 400 columns supported them, and of minarets framing every major part of the building, shows an aesthetic concern and a sense of the dramatic which are quite remarkable. Finally, all the main parts of the building exhibit a remarkable outer monumentality, which does not always correspond to the actual character of the interior (figs. 51–2 illustrate the point with respect to one of the domes in showing that the inner dome was smaller and different in type from the outer one). This monumentality and sense of showmanship have best been expressed by the medieval chronicler who wrote that 'its cupola would have been unique, had it not been for the heavens, and unique would have been its main arch, had it not been for the Milky Way' (Pugachenkova-Rempel, pp. 115 ff.).

52

The mausoleum known as *Ishrat-khaneh* (fig. 59) (House of Joy) has been attributed by popular legend to Tamerlane, but in fact was built by the wife of a later prince in 1464 as a mausoleum for Timurid women. The architectural importance of the building has been discussed by G. A. Pugachenkova in *Ars Orientalis*, vol. V (1963).

One of the most characteristic features of Timurid architecture — in which the Timurids were followed later by the Safavids and by the Uzbeks of Central Asia — was the creation of large monumental ensembles around an open square. The most spectacular of these is the *Registan* in Samarkand. Three major constructions remain around it. The first one is the *madrasah* of Ulugh beg, begun in 1420 (figs. 60–4); built on a classical four-*eyvans* plan, it has a magnificent façade and a superb decoration of tiles. The other two buildings are much later and replace abandoned or destroyed Timurid constructions. The *madrasah* Shir-dar was built in 1619–36; its façade (figs. 65–6) copies the portal of Ulugh beg's *madrasah* and a rather extraordinary method of supporting domes is found inside. The other late building, the so-called *Tilia-kari* (covered with precious metals) mosque and *madrasah* (figs. 67–70) was completed around 1660. Neither its plan nor its main features exhibit much originality and the heaviness of its forms contrasts with the elegance of earlier constructions.

The ensemble known as the *Shah-i Zindah* (King of Life) belongs to the group of monumentalized cemeteries which grew in many Near Eastern cities. The peculiarity of the one in Samarkand (fig. 71) is its location, on a hill, with a portal below and the mausoleums — together with small sanctuaries — lined up more or less regularly on either side of a narrow street. Cults had developed in this place as early as in the ninth century, and by the eleventh and twelfth centuries, constructions of one kind or another are known to have existed; but it is in the late fourteenth and in the fifteenth centuries that most of the present buildings were erected. The entrance was done by Ulugh beg (1434–5). The principal mausoleums are those of Shad-i Mulk Aka, a niece of Tamerlane who died in 1372 (figs. 79, 82), of Tuglu-Tekin (1376) (fig. 80), of Tuman aka, one of Tamerlane's wives (1405) (figs. 72–3), and of a khoja Ahmad (figs. 74–5). Many others are either undated or unnamed (figs. 76–8, 81–9), or else precise information on their identification has not been available. The importance of these mausoleums is manifold, but on two points they are of primary significance. First they illustrate a level of architecture which is not that of the great official monuments such as the *madrasahs* or the imperial tombs; they represent a more private type of religious-secular architecture with a greater emphasis on piety than on glory; they were often sponsored by others than the ruling princes and thus illustrate the taste and financial possibilities of lower segments of the aristocracy of the time. Second, because of their number in a comparatively short period, they provide us with a remarkable repertory of decorative designs and constructional techniques whose complete study is yet to be made.

Also in Samarkand the holy place known as *Abd-i Birun* ('Outer slave' as opposed to an 'inner' mausoleum within the walls of the city) (fig. 90) was erected in 1633 and illustrates a late rendition of Timurid architecture.

Shahr-i Sabz

The 'Green City' was an alternate capital for Tamerlane. At one time he thought of establishing his main capital there, and even after deciding on Samarkand as capital, he retained Shahr-i Sabz as a pleasure centre with gardens, parks, and palaces. A superb description of Tamerlane's palace there was given by the Spaniard Clavijo, but few monuments are left to justify his enthusiasm. The main one consists of a fragment — probably the gateway — of a palace construction known as Akserai (figs. 91–9) with massive forms recalling Ilkhanid monuments of north-western Iran. In addition there are at Shahr-i Sabz a number of memorial constructions, such as the mausoleum of Jehangir (figs. 100–1) built before 1394 and provided with a very curious triple dome (Rempel-Pugachenkova, p. 141), and two late mausoleums, the Kok Gunbadh (fig. 103) built in 1435–6 and the so-called Gunbadh-i Sayyidan (fig. 102) dated in 1437–8.

Turkestan

The city of Turkestan is celebrated for its remarkably well-preserved complex of buildings built in 1397 for a twelfth-century holy man, Khoja Ahmad Yassavi. It comprises a mosque, a mausoleum, a *khangah*, and a library. The whole forms an amazingly compact (figs. 104–9) structure with a superb decoration of tiles and of glazed bricks (figs. 110–11).

Uzgend

The city of Uzgend, deep in Ferghanah, is celebrated for an early minaret and for a remarkable group of three mausoleums set next to each other. Of these the most important are the northern one built for Jelal al-din al-Husayn in 1152 (figs. 112–13) and the southern one dated in 1187 (figs. 114–19). The two together provide us with one of the richest dictionaries of twelfth-century decorative motifs in Central Asia.

Urgench

In Urgench, one of the major ancient cities of Khorezm, are preserved several important mausoleums. The earliest seems to be the one in which Fakhr al-din Ghazi (d. 1208) is supposed to have been buried (fig. 122). The difficulty is that we know quite certainly that this personage died in Herat; hence the mausoleum is for all practical purposes anonymous and could be attributed to the end of the twelfth or the early thirteenth century. It is characterized by a remarkable simplicity of the main architectural forms. The second mausoleum is attributed on historical grounds to Tekesh, one of the ruling Khorezm-shahs of the early thirteenth century, and is much more complex in design (fig. 121). The third mausoleum, known as that of Turabek khanum (fig. 120) is datable in the third decade of the fourteenth century and has a very rare shape: it is twelve-sided on the outside and six-sided inside with an extensive façade. Most of its decoration has apparently been taken away, since its bare walls are quite unusual. It should be noted that this whole group of mausoleums has the very conical roofs which will be encountered again later in Anatolia and in Mosul.

Tirmidh

The city of Tirmidh was one of the main urban centres in the valley of the Oxus. Major excavations carried out there before and after World War II have brought to light a considerable amount of decorative stucco published in 1939 by B. Denike. Its remaining monuments are still little known (the most accessible statement is in *Akademiia Nauk Uzbek SSR, Trudy*, ser. 1, vol. 2, 1940), but the eleventh or twelfth century mausoleum illustrated here (fig. 123) shows an effective sobriety in the treatment of wall surfaces, which contrasts with the luxury of secular remains.

Ghujdawan

In this city, which is not too far from Bukhara, is found another *madrasah* ordered by Ulugh beg (figs. 124–5). It is dated in 1433.

Herat

The monuments of Herat have not yet been studied properly. Of the city walls, parts of which may go back to the twelfth century, the most spectacular remains consist of a bastion (fig. 136) soberly decorated with a monumental inscription in coloured brick. The main congregational mosque was first built in 1175–6; it was considerably rebuilt in later times, mostly in the fourteenth century, but in its hypostyle plan (fig. 130) and in many more or less easily visible details it exhibits features which are clearly early, perhaps even of the second half of the twelfth century. A final decision on their date, however, must await a more complete study of the monument than has hitherto been possible. The best known monuments of Herat belong to the fifteenth century, at a time when Gawhar Shad, Shah Rukh's wife, erected there a *madrasah*, a *musalla* (of which only a minaret remains, dated before 1437, fig. 133), and a magnificent mausoleum (figs. 126–7), decorated (figs. 128–9) with painting inside and tiles outside. The last of the great monuments of Herat is the *madrasah* of Husayn Bayqara (1469–1506), of which four of the 45-metres minarets are still standing (figs. 134–5).

Some two miles from Herat, at Gazur Gah, Shah Rukh built a sanctuary to a holy man, Khwajah Abd Allah Ansari. The sanctuary, which became the centre of a necropolis, is dated in 1428–9 and its decorative designs (figs. 137–42) are a sort of museum of motifs available to Timurid architects.

On the road from Herat to Kabul, at a place called *Chist*, there remain two very ruined mausoleums (figs. 143–4). No information seems to exist concerning their date or their purpose, but the magnificent stucco decoration of one of them suggests a date in the twelfth or early thirteenth centuries.

Ghazni

The so-called 'tower of Mahmud' (figs. 149–50) at Ghazni has been recently shown to be in fact a tower built between 1117 and 1149 for the Ghaznevid prince Bahramshah and to be later than the second tower of the same type inscribed with the name of Mas'ud III (1098–1115) (figs. 145–8) (J. Sourdel-Thomine, 'Deux minarets d'époque seljoukide,' *Syria*, vol. XXX (1953)). The purpose of these magnificent monuments, which were superbly decorated with brick work and stucco and which must be imagined with a cylindrical tower over the remaining polygonal ones, is still unclear. They have been called minarets or towers of victory.

Jam

The discovery by A. Maricq in 1957 of the capital of the Ghorids has been one of the more extraordinary events of the past decade. Located in a secluded valley of Afghanistan, it consists of many ruins which are still largely unexplored and of a sixty metres high minaret (fig. 151), datable by its inscription between 1153 and 1203 (A. Maricq and G. Wiet, *Le Minaret de Djam*, Paris, 1959). Although neither the exact architectural function of the minaret nor its specific purpose have as yet been worked out, the tenor of the inscriptions, especially the Koranic quotations, suggests that it was a commemorative monument of some sort (as well as a minaret), like the relatable Qutb al-Din minaret at Delhi, and it is possible that a commemorative meaning is to be given to most of these high towers in eastern Iran. The origin of the form is still obscure, although its development is undoubtedly related to the properties of brick architecture. The decoration of brick, stucco, and glazed tiles is of remarkable wealth and consists for the most part of several levels of geometric designs and of inscriptions.

Bust

Among the most remarkable ruined sites of Afghanistan is that of the ancient city of Bust extending over a huge area of Sistan. Two main fields of ruins are found there. The first one — the so-called Qal'ah-i Bust — contains the recently restored arch (figs. 152–4) of a probably twelfth-century mosque and a nearby brick construction (figs. 155–60), the Giyath al-din mausoleum which may have been part of the mosque. Both monuments have an important decoration of stucco, brickwork, and terra-cotta. The second area of ruins contains palaces of the Ghaznevid period which were partly restored in the twelfth century (figs. 161–2). This section of the site has been recently excavated by the French Archaeological Mission in Afghanistan (D. Schlumberger, 'Le Palais ghaznévide de Lashkari Bazar,' *Syria*, vol. XXIX (1952)).

Balkh

The great city of Balkh (Bactria) is one of the poorest in remaining monuments. Two sanctuaries — the shrine of Khwajah Akash (fig. 163) remarkably archaic in spite of its presumed Timurid date, and the superbly decorated shrine of the holy Khwajah Abu Nasr Parsa (figs. 164–6) built shortly after 1460–61 — are the only standing, even though ruined, buildings of the ancient metropolis. Nearby is found the 'minaret' of Dawlatabad (figs. 167–8), dated in 1108–9, according to the readings of the inscription made by Madame Sourdel-Thomine in a previously quoted article.

Sangbast

The major monument of Sangbast, near Mashhad, comprises an early minaret and a mausoleum supposed to be that of Arslan Jadhib, a Ghaznevid vizier who died in 1028 (figs. 169–70). The character of the structure justifies a date in the early eleventh century.

Tayabad

At Tayabad near the Persian-Afghan border there is a mausoleum to Zayn al-din; it is a construction (figs. 171–4) of the period of Shah Rukh (first half of the fifteenth century). Some of its faiences may be as late as 1565 although this conjecture has not yet been clearly ascertained.

Turbat-i-Shaykh-Jam

Near Tayabad is another mausoleum of considerable historical interest to the shaykh Ahmad al-Hasan; it has had a chequered history of destructions and rebuildings. The façade (fig. 175) is of the early fifteenth century.

Gunbadh-i Qabus

The Gunbadh-i Qabus (figs. 176–7) is dated in 1007 and is one of the most extraordinary monuments of early Islamic architecture. It was a tomb for a minor prince of north-eastern Iran; it was built in the prince's own life-time and serves not only as a mausoleum but also as a symbol of power. The striking purity of its almost undecorated brick walls is in complete contrast to that of most other monuments of this or later times. As a result it is still essentially an unexplained monument.

Hamadan

The Gunbadh-i Alaviyan in Hamadan is a simple square mausoleum (fig. 178) variously dated in the twelfth or the fourteenth centuries (with the latter perhaps more likely). It is provided both inside and outside (figs. 179–183) with one of the most complete ensembles of stucco decoration of any Iranian building. The themes of the decoration are striking because of their luxurious vegetal character.

Bistam

The ancient buildings of Bistam are all centred around the tomb of a local saint called Bayazid al-Bistami, who died around 878, and whose place of burial became a major centre for pilgrimages. Little by little a whole series of haphazardly planned buildings were added on. As long as no thorough survey is made of the remains, they cannot all be properly dated or explained. The earliest parts are dated by an inscription from around 1120 and include at least the minaret (fig. 184) and perhaps a few early walls. The rest (figs. 185–195) of the constructions were probably the work of Ilkhanid princes and are datable between 1299 and 1313.

Damghan

The city of Damghan is now, and was in the past, one of the major stopovers on the road from Khorasan westward. With the Tarik-khaneh (fig. 200), it boasts what is very likely the earliest remaining mosque in Iran, probably to be dated in the eighth or ninth centuries. In addition several early minarets have remained there, one (fig. 196) near the Tarik-khaneh datable before 1058, a second one by the main mosque datable around 1058 (fig. 197), and two cylindrical tombs, the mausoleum of Pir-i 'Alamdar (fig. 198) built in 1027 and the one called Chihil Dukhteran (fig. 199), constructed in 1056.

Yazd

The main congregational mosque at Yazd, in central Iran, is a complicated building with a long and involved history which has recently been masterfully reconstructed by M. Siroux ('Le masjid-é jum'ah de Yazd,' *Bulletin de l'Institut Français d'Archéologie Orientale au Caire*, vol. XLIV, (1947)). Parts of it go back to the twelfth century, but the illustrated details (figs. 204–6 and 209 and 219–20) all belong to the main period of rebuilding, between 1334 and 1365. A second building of the same period (around 1365) is commonly called the mausoleum of Shams al-Din, but is in fact a *madrasah* (figs. 207 and 208). Yazd also has several other sanctuaries, most of which remain unrecorded, except for a brief discussion of two of them by D. Wilber. These are the sanctuaries illustrated on figs. 201–3.

Saveh

The main monument of Saveh is the congregational mosque. Like so many monuments of central Iran, its core is of the twelfth century, and its minarets (figs. 212 and 214) are dated in 1110 and 1061. The proportions of its façade (figs. 211, 213) are also related to systems of proportion established in the twelfth century, although the work itself is, apparently, of the early sixteenth.

Tabriz

Tabriz was the capital of the Ilkhanid princes, but, unfortunately, not much has remained of its former glory. Of the principal buildings, one, the so-called Blue Mosque — now terribly damaged — is actually much later; it is dated in 1465 and in its superb decoration of coloured tiles (figs. 216–18) reflects something of the wealth of late fifteenth-century dynasties. Only the mosque of 'Ali Shah (figs. 219–20), built by a vizier of the Ilkhanid Oljaytu in 1310–20, with its extraordinary massive walls of brick without decoration, testifies to the greatness of the first Mongol empire.

Maraghah

To the north of the town of Maraghah, celebrated for the observatory built there by the Mongol Hulagu, there are five tower mausoleums of the twelfth through fourteenth centuries. They exhibit most of the available shapes and show an inventiveness of design on their outer walls with bricks, terra-cotta, and stucco which differentiates them from most of the central Iranian buildings. They are rather to be related to the equally superb mausoleums of Soviet Azerbayjan, especially from Nakhichevan. The main buildings are Gunbadh-i Surkh (fig. 223) dated in 1147; Gunbadh-i Ghaffariyah (figs. 221–2), dated in 1316–17; Gunbadh-i Kabud (figs. 224–5), dated 1196–7; Gunbadh Joi Burj (fig. 226), perhaps *ca.* 1330.

Nakhichevan

Among the most remarkable examples of architecture and decoration in Azerbayjan are the mausoleums in and around Nakhichevan. From 1161–2 dates the mausoleum of Yusuf b. Kathir (figs. 227–8), a simple octagonal structure with a polyhedral roof; its decoration of bricks, terracotta, and stucco still uses comparatively simple geometric forms. The Mu'minah Khatun mausoleum (1186–7), only a few years later, on the other hand, is outstanding for the growing complexity of its multiple decorative designs and for a far greater articulation of the surfaces of the walls (fig. 229). At Juga, some distance from Nakhichevan, stands another mausoleum, probably to be dated in the thirteenth century, whose squatness recalls contemporary Anatolian buildings, but whose decoration of complex geometric designs (figs. 231–2) is quite Iranian in spirit. At Barda another building, this time of the fourteenth century (figs. 233–4), is a simple round structure, whose polychrome brick decoration contrasts in its simplicity with the complex movement of the *muqarnas* in the doorway. Another fourteenth century mausoleum in the region, at Karabaglar (fig. 230), has a similar decoration of bricks but a monumental treatment of wall surfaces which recalls earlier experiments farther east. It is clear that the mausoleums of Azerbayjan form a distinctive group, both related to and separate from mausoleums of Anatolia and Iran. It is a curious thing that almost all of them have preserved the name of their architects, which would indicate a higher social position of the architect in Azerbayjan than elsewhere. For further references, see F. Sarre, *Denkmäler persischer Baukunst*, Berlin, 1910, and especially the convenient volumes published by the historical institute of the Azerbayjan Academy of Sciences, *Arhitektura Azerbayjana epoha Nizami*, Baku, 1947, and L.T. Bretanitskij and others, *Istoriia Arhitektury Azerbayjana*, Moscow, 1963.

Sultaniyah

The mausoleum of Oljaytu in Sultaniyah (figs. 235–6) is one of the most spectacular monuments of Ilkhanid architecture. It was the focal point of a new capital and was certainly erected during the life-time of the prince (1307–13). Its history, architecture, and decoration have been quite exhaustively dealt with in the *Survey of Persian Art* by A. Godard, who has discussed the extraordinary variety of the designs and techniques (figs. 237–46 and 248) found there as well as the peculiarities of the construction. Other mausoleums in the same city include the tomb of Chelebi Oglu (fig. 249) datable around 1330–3, and the tomb of Mullah Hasan (fig. 247) from the sixteenth century.

Qazvin

The two major buildings of Qazvin are the Haydariyah *madrasah*, whose *mihrab* is to be dated in the twelfth or thirteenth centuries and the congregational mosque (figs. 250 and 251), whose dome is dated in 1113, although the rest of the building is much later. The main prayer chamber and *mihrab* below the dome are also of the earlier date.

61

Rayy

Rayy, like Balkh, is one of the medieval cities about which we know much more from texts than from archaeological remains; the excavations which have been carried out at Rayy have not yet been published. Its much restored tomb (fig. 252) is usually dated in 1139, although the source for this dating is not absolutely certain.

Veramin

Veramin, near Rayy, was its immediate successor as the major city in the region, and has three remaining monuments of the early fourteenth century. Its congregational mosque (figs. 256–63), built in 1322–6, is a perfect example of a classical Persian plan. Its second monument is the tomb of Ala al-din (figs. 254–5), a typical heavy tower, dated in 1289. The third monument is an *imamzadeh* or funerary sanctuary built for an unknown holy man, Shah Husayn. The building has been dated around 1330, but the *mihrab* (fig. 253) may be later, perhaps from 1416–17, since a literary source mentions that date for the building (cf. Wilber, p. 177).

Natanz

The principal medieval building of Natanz, in central Iran, is a complex comprising a congregational mosque (fig. 272), a *khangah* (figs. 264–71), and the tomb of a holy man. The various parts are all dated between 1304 and 1325 and the remarkable portal of the *khangah* is dated in either 1316 or 1317.

Ardistan

The plan of the congregational mosque of Ardistan (figs. 273–6) is partly based on an early hypostyle building, of which a few elements remain, but most of the visible construction is clearly dated by inscriptions in 1158–60. It is one of the most important examples of the great Seljuq architecture of central Iran.

Nayin

The mosque of Nayin is one of the rare examples of a pre-Seljuq building in central Iran. Stucco reliefs (figs. 277 and 278) which clearly derive from Sasanian and early Islamic Mesopotamian designs, assign it to the tenth century.

Zavareh

The small town of Zavareh, also in central Iran, has two curious buildings. One, the congregational mosque, is the earliest (1135–6) known mosque with a plan of four *eyvans* around a courtyard. The second one, the *masjid-i Pa Minar*, is probably an Ilkhanid construction, although its minaret is dated in 1068–9. Both buildings have *mihrabs* of particular interest (figs. 279 and 280), the one in the congregational mosque being presumably of the same date as the mosque, while the one in the *masjid-i Pa Minar* is certainly earlier than the building and exhibits highly original decorative designs.

Gulpaygan

The dome chamber of the mosque of Gulpaygan (figs. 281–4) also belongs to the early twelfth century, while the rest of the mosque is of the nineteenth but, in the latter parts, a conscious effort has been made to maintain an earlier style of construction and of decoration.

Linjan

The sanctuary known as Pir-i Baqran, in the small village of Linjan south of Isfahan, has been repaired many times, but its central part was constructed between 1299 and 1312. Its extremely rich repertory of decorative motifs (figs. 287–95) makes it one of the most remarkable museums of Ilkhanid designs (cf. a detailed analysis by D. Wilber, pp. 121 ff.).

Ashtarjan

Ashtarjan, another small village in the area of Isfahan with a mosque dated around 1315–16, has been described in detail by D. Wilber (pp. 141 ff.). Like Pir-i Baqran it is remarkable for the wealth of its decorative designs (figs. 296–303). In addition the sanctuary of Rabi 'ah Khatun in the same village used to contain a *mihrab* dated in 1308 (fig. 308). This *mihrab* is now in the Teheran museum.

Isfahan

By all counts the congregational mosque at Isfahan was the masterpiece of the architecture of the Great Seljuqs in Iran. In spite of several studies, neither the history of the mosque nor a detailed survey of the existing structure is available, and considerable disagreement exists on the interpretation of the archaeological and literary sources which apply to the building. Limiting ourselves, then, to the photographs published here, we may say that the general conception of the façade on the court (figs. 304–5) is of the twelfth century, although most of the present decoration and the minarets are considerably later; that the walls shown on figs. 307 and 309 from the northern dome are certainly to be dated in 1088; that the *mihrab* on fig. 306 was ordered by the Ilkhanid Oljaytu and is dated in 1310; that the dates of the decorative designs on figs. 310 and 311 are probably Mongol or later. Among the other monuments of Isfahan illustrated here are the Do Minar Dardasht, a portal with two minarets and a tomb chamber (figs. 313, 315) datable between 1330 and 1340; the Chihil Dukhtaran minaret (fig. 317) dated in 1107; the *masjid* Ali minaret (fig. 316) built in the second half of the twelfth century or later (M. B. Smith, 'The Manārs of Isfahan,' *Athar-é Iran*, vol. I, 1936, p. 337); also the minaret of the Bagh-i Qush khaneh (figs. 314 and 318), of the fourteenth century. Like the minarets of the north-eastern part of Iran, these minarets — of which Isfahan has several other early ones — have not yet been fully explained either in terms of their significance within the monumental architecture of the city or as formal entities. Finally there is the main gateway (fig. 312) to the Deylamite mosque of Jo-jo or Jotjir founded by Sahib-i-Ibn-Abbad in the tenth century. If correctly dated, it is the only important remain in Isfahan of this period and was uncovered only in 1955 near the western gateway of the Hakim mosque.

Mashhad

We are still lacking both a complete history and a full description of the great sanctuaries in Mashhad, probably the holiest in the whole of Iran. One of the main religious institutions which was added to the holy tomb of Imam Rida, the shi'ite *imam* whose sepulchre sanctified the area, was the mosque which Gawhar Shad had completed in 1405–6 and which in its proportions (fig. 320) and in the details of its tile decoration (figs. 321–4) is one of the best examples of early fifteenth-century art.

Tus

The remarkable mausoleum known as the Haruniyah, at Tus, in north-eastern Iran (fig. 327), is still uncertainly dated. Earlier works (Pope in the *Survey of Persian Art*, pp. 1072–4; Wilber, pp. 145–6) have assigned it to the

SHAHR-I SABZ

Tilework on part of Tamerlane's palace, the Akserai

fourteenth century, but remarkable recent discoveries and studies concerning the monuments of medieval architecture in the southern part of Soviet Central Asia rather forcefully indicate an earlier date, perhaps even in the early twelfth century. The problem deserves a new analysis on the spot.

Erzerum

Erzerum, located high in the mountains (fig. 328), has always been a stronghold on a major road and hence the scene of many battles. It is all the more amazing to see then that some superb monuments have remained there, perhaps because for the first time in our survey we penetrate into an area of stone construction. The best known monument of Erzerum is the Cifte Minareli *madrasah*, built in 1253 by Huant Hatun, the daughter of a Seljuq prince. The superbly proportioned and composed (fig. 334) building has an extraordinary decoration on columns and on the portal (figs. 330-3, 335), where brick themes of Iranian origin are mixed with elements of local traditions. The Yakutiye *madrasah* (figs. 339-341) was built in 1310 and is partly in brick. In the citadel there may also be a few remains (lower part of fig. 336) of the thirteenth century, but in various parts of the town are found tombs (figs. 329, 337-8), the date of which is probably the thirteenth century, although some may be a little later. Most of the Erzerum examples are circular with a polygonal engaged arcade and with a high conical roof over a usually highly decorated cornice; in shape many recall certain Central Asian types.

Tercan

The small village of Tercan, some 120 kilometres west of Erzerum, possesses an unusual mausoleum, known as the Mama Hatun türbesi (figs. 342-8). A circular wall has a magnificent portal leading into a court in which stands the mausoleum itself.

Pozar

The caravanseraglio known as Hatun Han, near Pozar (between Amasya and Tokat) was built in 1238-9; like most other caravanseraglios it is particularly remarkable for its façade (figs. 349-51).

Amasya

Amasya was another city of major commercial and military importance, one of the first to have been conquered by the Seljuqs. The Halifet Gazi türbesi

E

65

(fig. 352) is dated around 1142–6 and was built for a vizier of the Danishmend dynasty; in 1209 a *madrasah* was added to the tomb. The Burmali Minare mosque (fig. 353) is dated in 1243. The Turumtay türbesi (fig. 355) was built in 1278–9; it is square and has very original decorative designs on the façade. Another late thirteenth-century tomb was erected over a mosque (fig. 354) and has the peculiarity of being in brick. Finally the so-called Bimarhane *madrasah* (figs. 356–9), dated in 1309, has a great number of decorative designs clearly imported from farther east.

Tokat

The Gök *madrasah* in Tokat was built in 1275 and heavily restored in 1930. Only a few fragments of its decoration (figs. 360–1) are left. The tomb of Nur al-din b. Sentimur with a handsomely severe portal (fig. 362) is dated in 1314 and is remarkable for having a curiously twisted pyramidal roof of brick.

Niksar

The Kirk Kizlar türbesi or mausoleum of the forty daughters is an early thirteenth-century building in brick, whose decoration (fig. 363) recalls Iranian designs, just as its name is related to the name of many Iranian sanctuaries.

Sivas

The principal monuments of Sivas (ancient Sebastia), one of the major strongholds of the Seljuqs of Anatolia, are all, curiously enough, nearly contemporary. The celebrated Gök *madrasah* was built in 1271–2 and its architect, Keluk b. Abdallah, was also responsible for one of Konya's buildings (fig. 410). Its most spectacular feature is a monumental façade (fig. 368) with side bastions, and a central gate flanked by two tall minarets. The Cifte Minareli *madrasah* is dated in 1272, but only its façade has remained with an equally elaborate decoration (figs. 366–7, 369–71). Finally the Muzaffer Bürüciye *madrasah* was also built in 1271–2. It is a less impressive building, but some of its decorative designs (figs. 365 and 372) have a quality of precision and detail more closely associated with Syria than with either Iran or Christian Armenia. There is in Sivas one older building, the hospital and tomb of Kai-kavus, built in 1217 of red bricks and decorated with blue tiles (figs. 373–4).

Van

The city of Van includes among its remains an anonymous thirteenth-century tomb (fig. 375), whose trilobed arcades have a curiously Western look.

Bitlis

In neighbouring Bitlis, a fragment of stone work (fig. 376) is probably Ottoman, but clearly shows the maintenance of earlier decorative themes.

Eski Malatya

The ancient city of Malatya is now almost uninhabited. Its main mosque dates from the thirteenth century for the most part and its gates are dated 1247 and 1273. Its remains (figs. 377–9) are curious in that they mix very Iranian brick features with Syrian stone work, and with interlaced tiles of Anatolian origin; in addition there is found there a strange and probably late pillar with magical symbols (fig. 380).

Ak Han

The Ak Han (near Goncali) was completed in 1253 and 1254. Here is preserved another example of a superb portal (figs. 381–2).

Diyarbakr

The Great Mosque of Diyarbakr (figs. 383–5) has been one of the most discussed buildings in Anatolian architecture. In plan it is of the early Islamic Syrian type, but it was almost entirely redone in the twelfth century, when ancient columns and capitals were used to create a façade on the court which is remarkably theatrical in appearance. On the outside occurs a rare instance of figural sculpture on a mosque. The meaning of this and other instances of Anatolian Seljuq figural sculpture is unclear, but probably is to be connected with various magical purposes.

Hosab

Although less well preserved than religious architecture, Anatolian secular architecture is quite noteworthy. The date of the gateway to the castle at Hosab (fig. 386) is uncertain but some of its re-employed stones may partly have been as early as the thirteenth century. Also important are several bridges (figs. 387–90), such as the 1146–7 one over the Batman Su, near Silvan.

Ahlat

At Ahlat, near Lake Van, several mausoleums are found. The two on fig. 391 are dated in 1281 and 1279 and served for burials of various princes and members of their families. Among later mausoleums, fig. 392 introduces a newly discovered one for a person by the name of Erzen hatun and dated in 1396–7, while fig. 393 shows a detail of the well-known Bayindir tomb (1491), with its open walls. Fig. 394 is another instance of the many anonymous mausoleums of the area, and fig. 395 illustrates the more elaborate Ulu tomb datable between 1273 and 1281.

Mardin

The most remarkable monument of the admirably situated town of Mardin is the *madrasah* of Sultan Isa (figs. 396–9), dated in 1385. Almost appearing to have been carved out of the rock, it is on two levels and exhibits superb stone construction together with a great variety of decorative designs, especially on the façade. The earlier Şehidiye mosque has been completely restored and only a few details (figs. 400–1) appear to go back to the thirteenth or fourteenth centuries. Outside of the town proper lies the late mausoleum of Sultan Hamzah (fig. 402), while the Great Mosque, founded in 1176 but much restored, has preserved an impressive early minaret (figs. 403–4).

Nisibin

The ancient town of Nisibin has few Muslim monuments, except for an undated wall fragment (fig. 405) in the courtyard of the old church of St. James and for a mosque which is probably a reconverted church.

Trebizond

In Trebizond the church of Hagia Sophia, probably built in the early thirteenth century, has a few fragments (figs. 408–9) of decoration clearly related to those of contemporary Muslim monuments. While these fragments show the contemporary impact of Seljuq ornament on non-Muslim buildings, figs. 406 (a fragment from the eighteenth-century castle at Dogan Bayazit) and 423 (window in a bath house at Meram) illustrate the preservation of the motifs.

Konya

Of all the great cities of Seljuq Anatolia, none is so rich in monuments as Konya, the ancient Iconium, which was during most of the thirteenth century the capital of the Seljuq state of Rum. Even though the secular buildings of the town have almost completely disappeared, a few fragments (figs. 412–13) illustrate the significant use of figural images in that architecture. The largest building in the city is the congregational mosque of Alaeddin, built at various times between 1155 and 1220 and containing a tomb in its courtyard (figs. 414–419). Its decoration is extensive and varied, although not so impressive as the decoration of Konya's other monuments. The Karatay *madrasah* and tomb, dated in 1251–2, has a curious portal (fig. 420) and a superb example of turquoise and dark purple tiles in the dome of the tomb (fig. 421), as well as interesting wooden doors (fig. 422). The often photographed Ince minaret and *madrasah*, dated in 1258 (figs. 410 and 411), has one of the most original façade decorations, which is not, however, overly attractive or even comprehensible. The Sahip Ata mausoleum (1282) and mosque (1279) offer some of the best examples of Anatolian tile work (figs. 433 and 434), although the buildings themselves are partly ruined. The Sircali *madrasah* (1242), a royal foundation, is interesting in that one of its builders was from Tus in eastern Iran and its designs (figs. 426–8) have been related to Iran. Among the later monuments of the city are the *tekke* of the whirling dervishes (fig. 424) and an institution for people who wanted to memorize the Koran, dated in 1421 (fig. 425). Some twenty kilometres outside of Konya lies the superb *han* of Sa'd al-din, built in 1235–6, which is particularly remarkable for the sobriety of its stone façade and for the re-use in it of many antique stones (figs. 429–32).

Karaman

Karaman, south of Konya, was the centre of one of the most powerful Anatolian emirates of the late Middle Ages. The building of Ibrahim bey (1426–62) exemplifies the continuity of Seljuq patterns and plans (figs. 437–9). The Hatuniye *madrasah* (1382), built on a fairly classical plan, still shows the extraordinary decorative wealth (figs. 440–6) so characteristic of thirteenth-century architecture (compare fig. 446 with fig. 372), but with considerable differences in style, in particular with respect to the precision, even obviousness of the design. The same point can be made about the decoration of the Kizlar tomb (*ca.* 1487) (figs. 447–9).

Beyşehir

In Beyşehir the Eşrefoglu mosque and tomb, dated in 1298, has an interesting gate (fig. 450), a door of carved wood (fig. 451), and a tomb with a dome covered with turquoise and blue floral designs (fig. 452).

Niğde

In Niğde, the 1224 Alaeddin mosque has a portal (figs. 453–4) related to examples seen elsewhere in Anatolia, but with an interesting variant in the high decorative arch. The Sunghur bey mosque (1338) still exhibits similar designs, and shows in addition a western influenced rose-window (figs. 455–6). The Khudavand tomb (1312) is of a typical shape (fig. 457), but with an excellent portal (fig. 458) and a rather curious series of sculpted fragments. The Ak *madrasah* (1409) also shows the preservation of thirteenth-century themes (figs. 459–60).

Akserai

The Sultan Han, near Akserai, is one of the most sumptuous secular constructions which has remained from the Islamic Middle Ages. Most of it was built between 1229 and 1279, although a few additions were made in the fourteenth century. Among its peculiarities is the jewel-like ornament of its façade and of the edicule in its main courtyard (figs. 461–2).

Silvan

The great mosque of Silvan (medieval Mayafariqin) has had a complicated history. Most of its features are of the first half of the thirteenth century and show the impact of Syria in the minaret (fig. 465) and of Iran in the *mihrab* (fig. 464).

Agzikara Han. Various caravanseraglios

This Han (between Akserai and Nevsehir) is another of the great caravanseraglios of Anatolia, datable between 1236 and 1246, with the same characteristics of portal decoration and of wall corners lined with carved designs (figs. 466–9). Perhaps the greatest of these was the Sultan Han near Kayseri, datable *ca.* 1232–6, in which (figs. 470–6) the variety of designs is particularly stunning and curiously close (fig. 474) to certain themes of northern nomadic art. Also not far from Kayseri is Karatay Han, built between 1230 and 1240 and with the usual wealth of decoration (figs. 487–94). In the area of Akserai is found Alay Han (fig. 505), datable perhaps as early as in the late twelfth century, while Evdir Han (fig. 509) and Sari Han (figs. 507–8) belong respectively to a period between 1215 and 1219 and to the middle of the thirteenth century.

Kayseri

The city of Kayseri is, after Konya, the richest in buildings of the thirteenth century. The Ali Ja'far tomb (1247–8) (fig. 477), the magnificent complex of buildings (mosque, *madrasah*, tomb) known as Huand Hatun (1237–8) (figs. 479, 482–4), the Cifte *madrasah* (1206) comprising in fact two *madrasahs* and a mausoleum (fig. 481), the Sahibiye *madrasah* (1268) (fig. 486), and the heavily decorated Döner mausoleum (1276) (fig. 485), are all examples of the remarkable skill of the stone masons and decorators of the thirteenth century.

Divrig

Divrig boasts some of the most original Seljuq buildings. While the Sitte Melik Türbe (1196) (fig. 495) is closely related to mausoleums mentioned before, the main façade of the Ulu Cami (fig. 497) has an overwhelming decoration which is quite obviously exaggerated and yet rather effective by its sheer mass, while the eastern façade (fig. 500) is more traditional. The Ulu Cami is attached to a hospital (fig. 496), which has a characteristic façade. In the citadel an early (1180–1) mosque (figs. 499, 501) was built by an architect from Maraghah.

Ercis

At Ercis and Gevas, near Lake Van, are a number of mausoleums datable in the thirteenth or perhaps early fourteenth centuries (figs. 502–4, 506).

Aleppo

The city of Aleppo was on the crossroads of paths to and from northern Mesopotamia, Palestine, Egypt, and Anatolia. Hence it is no accident that one of its most remarkable monuments is a much repaired citadel (figs. 519–20), whose main part belongs to the late twelfth century and to most of the thirteenth. The minaret of the congregational mosque (fig. 518) belongs to the eleventh century and is the earliest monument of Seljuq architecture in Syria. The Zahiriyah (figs. 516, 517) *madrasah*, dated in 1223, as well as the *madrasah* al-Firdaws (1235) (figs. 515, 521), are excellent examples of the sober architecture of northern Syria, while the 1403 al-Utrush mosque (figs. 522-3) represents the much more decorated style of the late Mamluk period inspired from Egypt.

Dunaysir (mod. Kiziltepe)

Also on the road from Iran westward was the town of Dunaysir in which a superb mosque was built in the year 1200 (figs. 510-11, 512-13). The simplicity of the lines of its façade are in curious contrast with the wealth of the *mihrab* decoration.

Delhi

The celebrated Qutb minaret (fig. 524) built in 1206 is more than a monument to call for prayer, being a spectacular symbol of the new faith in India. It should now be related to the newly discovered Jam minaret in Afghanistan (A. Maricq and G. Wiet, *Le Minaret de Djam*, Paris, 1959).

Ajmir

The mosque at Ajmir (figs. 525-7) shows the translation of Iranian architecture into Indian stone. It was begun around 1200 and is known as the *Arhai-din-ka-Jhompra* (hut of two-and-a-half days), presumably because it used to be on the site of a fair that lasted two and a half days.

III. ARCHITECTURE AND DECORATION

Like most of the problems posed by Islamic art and culture, the question of the growth and character of Islamic architectural decoration has never been discussed in its entirety; the only works written on the subject have either dealt with limited areas (such as the studies by L. I. Rempel and B. P. Denike on Central Asia) or discussed specific techniques or themes (such as D. Wilber's study of mosaic faience decoration or Shafi'i's analysis of the calyx-shaped floral design). And even these more limited and more detailed studies have not been sufficiently numerous to permit many generalizations. The remarks presented here are, therefore, not meant to be either a history of architecture and decoration — which would be impossible at this stage of our knowledge — or

even an aesthetic of Islamic decoration since we have so few theoretical foundations on which to build any sort of aesthetic approach to Islamic art. All they
are meant to be are random thoughts which may help to bring some order into
the accumulated mass of available material and to prepare the ground for
further discussion and explanation.

1. THE TECHNIQUES

The first two techniques of decoration involved the medium of construction
itself. In Anatolia, where the traditional medium of construction was stone,
carved stone became the major medium for ornamentation. The technique is a
very ancient one and does not require further elaboration, except on one specific
point: in many instances the stone sculpture seems to have been applied to the
surface of the wall rather than understood as an intrinsic part of the fabric of
the wall; it often appears remarkably artificial, as though it was imitating something else.

Much more original than the medieval Islamic use of stone is the use made
of bricks for decorative as well as constructional purposes. The origins, significance, and development of this ornamental 'brick style' are still somewhat of a
puzzle, because its earliest clear example (figs. 1 and 2) is also its most perfect
example, in the sense that, except for the dome, not one part of the building
escapes the ambiguity of being meaningful on two levels: as decorated surfaces
as well as parts of architectural volumes such as walls, towers, or spandrels of
arches. In later centuries, although brick was no longer the only technique of
decoration, it remained as a major one and the number of uses to which it was
put increased considerably. Variations in brick work came not merely to
emphasize the major architectural lines of the building (f. i. fig. 149), but also to
distinguish the surfaces to be ornamented. The manner of laying bricks trans-
forms into a linear zigzag pattern the curved surfaces of a dome (fig. 169).
In many minarets (figs. 11, 12, 196) or tombs (fig. 199), it is brick which gives
its texture to the walls; in the richer examples the device which was used consisted in creating decorative designs by the very manner in which bricks were
laid; in simpler instances bricks were separated from each other by an interstice
of varying size (figs. 199, 193, 119, 77) which could be left open or filled with
stucco designs, but which in both cases gave a sense of volume to the wall. In
some instances (fig. 298) the effect of this brick work was artificially created
in stucco. Examples did exist (figs. 219–20, 176–7) where the brick was used
in its full purity and superb masses of brick work were composed, but these

instances remain comparatively rare. The main interest and the historical significance of brick as ornament are that, even though its origins are not very clear, its gradual spread from the cities of Central Asia to the rest of Iran and even to Anatolia (fig. 341, for instance, and there are other examples) can clearly be established as one of the principal characteristics of the eleventh and subsequent centuries, and also that, even in the monuments of the seventeenth century, for instance in Bukhara, the ornamental possibilities of the medium of construction were never forgotten.

The third technique of architectural decoration is not peculiar to Iran alone, but may have originated there and certainly found there some of its most remarkable uses: it is stucco. Already in pre-Islamic times, whether in western Iran and Iraq, as at Ctesiphon, or in eastern Iran, as at Varahsha, or in Central Iran, as at Rayy, stucco had been used to cover walls of palaces and temples, because the medium of construction — rubble in mortar or unbaked brick — was not very impressive and also because richness of surface decoration was deemed to create a more important effect than barren walls. Although instances do exist (as in the palace of Sarvistan) where stucco was simply applied to the walls without major decoration, in most cases an extensive sculpture is found on these walls, using decorative themes issued from textiles and iconographically significant images to create in cheap material an impression of magnificence. These early Iranian themes and purposes were picked up by the Muslims as early as in the eighth century and characterize the stuccoes of the Umayyad palaces of Syria and Jordan, or, in a more original way, those of Samarra. At Nayin, in the tenth-century section of the mosque (fig. 277; cf. also fig. 275), something of the character of older themes of decoration in stucco can be still found. It is interesting to note than these very same earlier modes and themes are found as late as the eleventh century in secular architecture, for instance in Tirmidh, which unfortunately could not be illustrated here.

The history of stucco is thus continuous, and by the eleventh century the medium existed throughout the Near East, basically as a mode to cover the walls with decorative designs. But considerable changes were brought into the appearance of stucco some time in the eleventh century, although any precise date is quite arbitrary, given our limited knowledge of the period. These changes were partly in the themes that were used, and to these we shall return; but there were also changes in the manner in which stucco was used. The old function of wall covering is there (figs. 180, 182, 190, etc.), but in most instances the stucco is not simply applied to the wall but organized according to a series of major architectural lines; a similar subservience to architectural principles occurs in

74

such instances as were mentioned before, where brick surfaces are imitated in stucco. Finally stucco is also used in interstices (fig. 259) between bricks or (fig. 275) as a sort of decorative veil over the simple structure of the vault. From Iran this versatility in the possibilities available to stucco was carried elsewhere, although in the great architectural compositions of Anatolia, stucco themes were more often copied into stone, which is probably responsible for the somewhat artificial character of some of them. In later architecture, stucco became a nearly indispensable aid supporting and enlivening other, more exciting, techniques.

The fourth significant medium of decoration was more peculiar to the Iranian sphere. It consists of terra-cotta, i.e., basically, of ceramic fragments that were specially moulded or formed to fit certain areas or to develop certain patterns. It was, in other words, an applied decoration which was more expensive than stucco and which created greater relief in designs and especially greater contrasts between different types of designs. The technique was already known in Parthian times in Central Asia and it is in Central Asia and in Afghanistan that we see it reappear in the Middle Ages — as at Uzgend (fig. 114) or Qal'ah-i Bust (fig. 154); new instances of the use of the technique in central Iran are constantly coming to light, as in the eleventh-century northern dome at Isfahan.

The most important development related to this use of ceramic in architectural decoration is what has been called 'mosaic faience'. Its basic aim is clear enough, the introduction of colour, and it is this colour which, even in black-and-white photographs, gives to the great monuments of the fifteenth century in Samarkand (figs. 33 ff.) or Mashhad (fig. 320) as well as to the superb Safavid or Ottoman buildings of a later period, their unique quality. As D. Wilber has shown, the full development of colour on the surface of walls took place at the very time when, in the fourteenth century, the older techniques of stucco and brick began to lose their effectiveness (for a rather weak example see fig. 306). But the idea of using colour at all was not an idea of the fourteenth century. As early as the middle of the eleventh century, at Damghan (figs. 196–197), the letters of the inscriptions were glazed. At Maraghah (figs. 223 ff.) colour is used to identify the main lines of the decoration. The technique of using colours on otherwise identifiable elements of construction or decoration in order to stress certain lines or certain parts of the buildings or of the decoration will remain a constant characteristic of Islamic architecture (figs. 24, 304, 434 among many possible instances of late buildings) and its origins must probably be sought in a universal tradition of using painting to emphasize certain architectural or decorative details; many examples exist of stuccoes with painted backgrounds and even painted motifs of decoration.

But, if the first use of colour is fairly easy to explain technically and historically, the next stage is less so. Whole surfaces were covered with multicoloured tiles which developed certain designs independently of architectural needs and, in the most complete examples, were used alone, and not in combination with other techniques such as stucco or brick. The technical varieties of such tiles and their schools have usually been discussed in histories of ceramics, and need not concern us here, but the origins of the technique as a whole have been a matter of some discussion. It is in the monuments built in Konya in the middle of the thirteenth century (figs. 421, 433) that faience mosaic on large wall surfaces appears for the first time in full. This poses the problem whether it is a local Anatolian development or whether it is merely the Mongol invasions which pushed Iranian artists into Anatolia and permitted them to create there what they would have created in Iran anyway. Since both Turkish and Iranian architecture of later centuries used the techniques, whereas in the Arab countries of Syria and Egypt it was clearly only a foreign importation, it may perhaps be concluded that the discovery of the possibilities offered by coloured tiles belongs to both regions. The ultimate possibility of coloured tile decoration was to transform completely an architectonic composition into a brilliant combination in which architectural masses, decorative designs, and colour combined with each other while at the same time each of these elements had its own principles and characteristics. Within the range covered by the plates of this book, it is in the Timurid monuments of eastern Iran that the most perfect balance between all these elements was achieved. The potential danger of the technique is similar to the danger of stucco, i.e., that, even though it requires a wall in order to be, its effectiveness is to an extent independent of the quality of the architecture on which it is used and in more than one instance there is something absurd in the development in some secondary corner of an entrance way of a superb panel of coloured tiles.

Finally Muslim architects used painting, wood carving, glass, marble, and alabaster, but these techniques have not left us enough examples to judge of their original impact, even though some of them, such as wood, were quite important in the growth of the better preserved techniques. A few instances of the use of each of these techniques are visible in the plates.

2. THE THEMES OF DECORATION

In so vast a region as the one with which we are dealing there are bound to be considerable differences from one province to the other. The artistic background as well as the technical possibilities of Anatolia or of Khorasan were so different that any similarity between them would seem unlikely. And the differences are great indeed. Yet it is perhaps even more remarkable that similarities do exist and that relationships can be established between various parts of the Near Eastern Islamic world. Before pointing out some of the most common and most obvious of the themes used by medieval architects, a word must be said about the character of the most constantly decorated parts of buildings.

If one excepts the earliest monuments, such as the tomb of the Samanids, in which decoration and architecture were totally blended, the sequence of early minarets (figs. 10–11, 13, 125, 133–4, 145–50) with brick or terra-cotta completely transforming the cylindrical surface of the building, and some of the more spectacular Timurid monuments of Samarkand (figs. 31 ff.) or Mashhad (figs 320 ff.) and Herat (figs. 126 ff.), where coloured tiles are used all over the surface of the walls (or at least involved all sections of the walls), there are two parts of the religious buildings illustrated here which consistently display a particularly spectacular decoration. The point is especially true for the twelfth and thirteenth centuries, at the heyday of the period with which we are dealing. These two parts are the entrance and the *mihrab*. Since they form the most characteristic decorated elements of the medieval Islamic building, the great ornamental ensembles of Islamic architecture, it is necessary to explain briefly their function and their growth.

An explanation is all the more necessary since they had not been from the very beginning show places of ornament and design. In early Islam, the *mihrab* was a commemorative niche related either to the person of the prince and *imam* or to the place where the Prophet used to stand while leading prayers. In either instance our early examples of *mihrabs* show rather simple niches and it was only little by little that the *mihrab* became a sort of focal point of the decoration of the mosque. A dome was often built in front of it, and gradually the *mihrab* became a symbolic theme of eschatological writing as well as the inspiration for decorative designs on tombstones and prayer rugs. The exact history of this development is obscure, although the Samarra monuments of the ninth century and those of Cordova in the tenth indicate already that something more profound than the mere commemoration of an early Islamic moment was involved in the *mihrab*; it is at that time that the niche on the back wall of the mosque's hall of prayers began to assume a preponderance that found one of its most magnificent and almost absurd fulfilments in the huge *mihrab* of the Dunaysir mosque (its size is hardly scaled to the building) (fig. 510). It may also be pointed out that, as the main *mihrabs* grew in size and appeared in larger and larger halls,

77

the movement toward private piety which has been mentioned as a characteristic feature of much of the Islamic world from the twelfth century on, led to the creation of smaller private *mihrabs* which might be built into a column or on a side wall. These could serve a smaller group of faithful to gather for quiet prayer, or they could serve to express an individual's faith. In all instances, however, the *mihrab* consisted of a central arched area (usually, but not always, concave) with decorative embellishments within the *mihrab* and in the frame which was provided for the arch; usually this frame consisted of a series of bands of varying widths with other decorative themes filling the spandrels.

The development of the gate is somewhat similar. In Bukhara's earliest monument the four entrances are hardly distinguishable from the rest of the building. But already in the second oldest building of the city (fig. 3) there begins to develop a more monumental entrance. The example is of the twelfth century and at Qal'ah-i Bust (fig. 152) we may be dealing with an even earlier instance. The curious feature in the development of the monumental gateway is that it existed from the very beginning in the secular architecture of Islam. It is, however, only slowly that mosques acquired it and it is probably under the influence of royal architecture that monumental gates begin to appear, for instance at Cordova. It is possible indeed that princely patronage was also involved in the gates which developed in Iran, Syria or Anatolia in the twelfth century. But another factor, not unrelated to the purposes of princely gates, may have also influenced their development in religious architecture. It is a curious fact that the mausoleums (fig. 120) were among the first monuments to acquire most spectacular gates; they are even at times transformed into entrance complexes which almost overshadow the sepulchral hall itself. The tradition of such gates continued well into the fifteenth century, since the Shah-i Zindah in Samarkand (fig. 71) has almost the appearance of a succession of gates and domes. Why should the mausoleum have developed to such an extent the *pishtaq*, the 'front arch' so typical of later Iranian architecture? A possible explanation may be that, just as the palace gate symbolized the sacred and forbidding royal city behind it, so the gate of the mausoleum extends, by its very size and beauty, something of the grace and holiness of the personage buried in the tomb. And, one may suppose that, not unlike Western cathedrals, the sanctuaries of holy men in one city competed with those of other cities and that gates were among the most obvious features by which one sanctuary could triumph over the other. Whatever the original reasons, the monumental entrance became a standard feature of Islamic buildings from the eleventh century on, and secular or religious buildings were consistently provided with them. Often, as in Anatolian caravanseraglios or in Syrian *madrasahs* (fig. 516) they formed almost the only highly decorated part of the building. At other times, as at Divrig (fig. 497) or Sivas (figs. 366–9) in Anatolia and as at Turkestan (fig. 110) or Samarkand (figs. 60 or 66) the whole façade of the building was included in the composition whose centre was the monumental gate. The shapes of these gates varied considerably from simple recessed *eyvans* with comparatively straight lines (fig. 60) to a most remarkable complexity of planes and recesses (figs. 118, 297, 312, 332, etc.). Whether using flat surfaces or complex combinations of planes, the gates and the adjacent areas which combined with them to make up the decorative unit challenged the artist to discover means of creating designs that would give relief, brilliance, and excitement to these most visible parts of the buildings. It is a sign of the variety of inspiration and taste available to Muslim architects that such fascinatingly different monuments were achieved as the organized wealth of the entrance to Bibi Khanum's *madrasah* (fig. 41) in Samarkand and the rather crazy accumulation of Divrig's mosque (fig. 497). But in both these instances, as in most other cases, certain basic features, specifically pertaining to the gate and yet also not unrelated to the *mihrab*, such as a central void, side walls, and a rectangular frame, remained consistently characteristic of the medieval Muslim gate.

To the *mihrab* and to the gate one could easily add as characteristic ensembles the minaret or the circular and polygonal tombs; each of these forms posed its own architectural and decorative problems; all deserve study, but the two which have been singled out are the most common.

If we turn now to the central themes of ornament, these can perhaps best be divided into five basic elements, it being understood that in most instances, it was a combination of two or more of these elements which actually made up the design.

The first category is the rarest. Human and animal features existed in medieval Islamic sculpture; no examples *in situ* remain from Iran at the time of our monuments and the exact architectural function of the many stucco figures which are found in museums today is not very clear. A few instances of sculpture of human beings and mostly of animals exist in Anatolia (figs. 333, 380, 385, 412–13, 498), even on the walls of religious buildings; some of the subjects copy antique sculpture, others may have had some totemic significance, but, on the whole, neither the origins nor the significance at the time of this sculpture have yet been completely understood.

A second decorative theme may be called architectural. It is a known feature

79

of Islamic art that a considerable number of elements that had originally a structural meaning were transformed into purely decorative devices and as such played a part in vast ornamental compositions. Such elements are columns, single or in branches, and mouldings recombined in a peculiarly unarchitectonic fashion (figs. 352, 414, 497), or strange conglomerations of pilasters (figs. 118 or 119, 222), capitals, bases (figs. 164–6). But the single most common architectonic element in decoration is the so-called *muqarnas*, stalactite or honeycomb, which occurs first on the upper part of the minaret on fig. 10 and last on the capitals of the engaged columns on fig. 511, and on almost every figure in between. The *muqarnas* is an architectural and decorative element whose origins are as unclear as its ubiquity is certain. Basically it is a section of vault which, used in combination with other identical or related elements, creates a three-dimensional ornamental effect which can be scaled to any need, from vast niches (fig. 186) or entrances (fig. 505) to the smallest details of construction or decoration. In early times — such as the eleventh and twelfth centuries — examples exist to show that some *muqarnas* combinations had structural significance, but quite soon the possibility of creating surfaces of decoration at intersecting angles became the predominant concern, and a fake net of stucco (fig. 266) was often created for the sole purpose of permitting a greater number of decorative designs. At times a curious ambiguity remains as to whether certain combinations of forms were meant to be fully decorative or purely architectonic (figs. 128–9), an ambiguity which is present as early as in the tenth century in Cordova and Bukhara and which seems to complicate even further any attempt at defining precisely the significance of decoration in Islamic art.

A third theme of ornamentation was quite clearly geometry. The most common way in which geometry was used was in the creation of the basic patterns of design. At first glance, the tremendous variety of geometric shapes, rectangles (fig. 150), squares (fig. 148), various kinds of diamonds (figs. 139 and 142), an endless variety of geometrically conceived star patterns (figs. 153, 360), various 'net' patterns based on geometric principles (figs. 2, 171, 173), meanders (figs. 179, 347–8), and many circles, all seem to show the most amazing imagination and inventiveness. A recent study on Central Asian ornaments has shown that practically all the geometric designs can be achieved simply with a ruler and with a compass and that almost all designs can be reduced to a series of comparatively simple geometric shapes. The extent to which the point is true in the ornament of other Islamic areas still remains to be studied. The more significant facts about the geometric units used seem, how-

Ilkhanid tilework on the outside wall of the mausoleum of Oljaytu at Sultaniyah

ever, to be, first, their constant mobility in time and space, for in early designs such as those of Uzgend (figs. 112 ff.) we find basically the themes of Samarkand or Turkestan two hundred years later or even, translated into stone, those of Anatolia (figs. 365, 376, 382, etc.) two thousand miles away; and second that the fascination of the use of geometry in these designs is that in many instances (figs. 117, 153) the visible decoration is only a segment of the geometric design that was necessary for its creation.

The fourth theme of decoration was writing, the most ambiguous of them all, for it was the only one of these themes which had, in a sense, an iconographic significance. Koranic passages, eulogies to builders, or triumphal inscriptions served to explain the function of buildings or of parts of buildings and to perpetuate the pious memory of the founder. Inscriptions could point out the exact purpose in any given instance of plans and elements of construction which were, in different buildings, made to serve different functions, and this may in part explain the lavishness of their use, as well as their variety. Their range runs from the severe Kufic of the tomb of Qabus (fig. 177) to the superbly artificial squares in which certain traditional religious formulas were made more magical than understandable (fig. 89), from the simple statement (fig. 442) in cursive on a small cartouche to the monumentalization of the cursive (figs. 111 or 403) over large wall surfaces or to the playful mixture of writing with other decorative themes (figs. 141, 88, 398). Under all these formal guises, each of which has its own history, writing appears as an inescapable motif of Islamic architecture, like the statues of medieval churches, whose meaning is often lost to all but the initiated, but without which the cathedrals would have lost some of their precise identification in the past and much of their attraction today.

The last of the major decorative themes of this period consisted of vegetal elements. It is rarely indeed that one finds at this time any instance of a natural vegetation, of natural flowers or leaves. Yet at the same time there is hardly a panel of tiles (fig. 64) or a stone (figs. 441–2) that lacks some sort of vegetal element — mostly various modifications of the palmette, although other floral designs appear also. It would, however, be a mistake to consider Islamic vegetal ornament only from the point of view of the varying degrees of naturalism which appear in its leaves or flowers. For, in a deeper way, the true significance of vegetal themes was that they gave a tremendous sense of nervous life to the ornament. This appeared in two ways. First, so often, the tendril appears more striking than the leaf or the flower. And, second, in most instances, Muslim decorators did not use sterile vegetal motives; they gave them constant movement, either by relating them to the flow of writing (fig. 372) or by developing

F

them in a kind of whirl of moving tendrils and leaves (figs. 365, 370, 371). The point is particularly true in Anatolia, where (figs. 331, 497) Georgian and Armenian art brought a rude sense of vegetal themes absent from Iranian models. But even in Iran at Mashhad (fig. 320), on the *mihrabs* of central Iran (figs. 280, 279, 274), or on the stuccoes or tiles of Central Asia (fig. 119, 109, 98), the vegetal forms are superbly alive, with perhaps in the latter examples more of a rug-like brilliance than the power so typical of carved stone.

Other themes of decoration are found as well, for instance curiously abstract designs (figs. 513, 494, 482, 472), which do not readily fit into any of our categories. But rather than make a complete list of themes, it is perhaps more important to note that the peculiar wealth of the architectural decoration of these monuments derives from two main facts: first, it is a rare monument indeed in which any one of these themes appears alone, and second, all of them have both a concrete and an abstract meaning. Animals or human figures are decorative and magical; architectural themes are both supports for decoration and decorative in themselves; geometric elements have the same double function; writing is ornament and also meaning; vegetation is both artificial and lively. It is clear enough that Islamic art at this time had already developed a syntax of ornamentation which exceeds by far the accumulated richness of its morphological components. But a full understanding of the history or significance of either morphology or syntax must await the publication of these painstaking detailed monographs which are so sorely missing in Islamic art.

3. MEANINGS

As one peruses images of the Islamic architecture which established itself from Central Asia to Anatolia after the eleventh century, a curious ambiguity arises which may best be compared to the effects created by those books or films created ten to twenty years ago, which produced different impressions, according to whether one used special glasses to look at them. The mosque of Bibi Khanum (fig. 43), the Turkestan mosque (fig. 107), the mausoleum of Oljaytu (fig. 235) or one of the Anatolian Sultan Hans (figs. 466–76) — to name but a few instances from different areas and different periods — seem on the one hand to be magnificent compositions of masses in which the most architectonic values of space and volume were fully realized. Yet all these buildings, as one moves nearer (figs. 45, 110, 248, 471) appear also as flat wall surfaces in which a decoration using many different techniques and designs suddenly defeats the monumentality of the whole building. One can, of course, consider the phenomenon as a contradiction, and assume that Islamic patrons of the time were unable to decide whether they wanted permanent constructions utilizing the techniques and inventions of centuries of architectural traditions in the Near East or whether they preferred the more ephemeral brilliance of a superb wall or of an artificial *muqarnas*, in the way that one may prefer beautiful rugs or hangings to the purity of a solid wall. And in the past philosophical and mystical reasons derived from Islamic philosophy and mysticism were given to explain the fascination of so much of Islamic art with decoration.

And yet one may wonder whether to see in these monuments a clash between decorative and architectonic values, with the latter usually on the losing side, is not to misinterpret the elements which went into the making of this architecture. Clashes existed, no doubt, especially in some of the more absurd Anatolian façades (figs. 497 or 411), but they were not so much arguments between architecture and decoration as between a specific architectural tradition and a specific type of decoration. There is an exuberance in the great façades of Seljuq Anatolia, which exemplifies the complexity of the cultures which created Seljuq Anatolia and the bewilderment of patrons and architects as they had to choose between the wealth of local Armenian and Byzantine, imported Iranian and Syrian, perhaps also Turkish Central Asian traditions. The point is, however, that no national spirit or abstract Islamic ideology is responsible for the peculiar relationship of decoration and architecture which characterized Islamic architecture in the eleventh through fifteenth centuries in the area we have described. No such abstract conceptions can define or explain it, because most provinces had varying ethnic characteristics over the ages and also because the nature and meaning of piety also varied considerably from region to region and from century to century. Just as Baroque or Gothic catholicism varied from each other and at any one time in the various countries it affected, so it was at various moments of Islamic history, although perhaps to a lesser degree. This is not to say, of course, that no continuities existed or that no unity is found in various moments or areas of Islamic architecture. Seljuq Isfahan, Timurid Samarkand, Uzbek Bukhara, and Seljuq Anatolia, all have certain common features and all exemplify certain common interests and attitudes, such as the use of similar themes and techniques and a concern for the relationship between architecture and decoration. But since neither the permanence of an immobile Islam nor common ethnic sources can explain these elements of unity, one must look elsewhere.

In attempting here to make a few concluding remarks on the subject of what precisely this relationship was, we are obviously entering into a realm of hypotheses and doctrines somewhat beyond the pale of scholarship, inasmuch as there is no theoretical framework for the study of ornament any more recent than Riegl's old *Stilfragen* so often used by Islamic art historians, nor are there adequate specific studies of identifiable details from one area or the other — with the very few exceptions mentioned above. One can do no more than to suggest a few ideas which may help to explain what happened. Whether acceptable or not, and especially if they are not, these suggestions may incite others to do further work in this little-trodden field.

The first point to be made is that, regardless of the purposes of the buildings shown here, their patrons were in almost all instances princes, and the aim of the buildings became tied to their tastes. About this taste as it existed in the eleventh and twelfth centuries we are poorly informed, but the few texts which are known and the two or three actual examples of secular architecture indicate that the central wealth of secular buildings consisted of a multiplicity of objects, rugs, paintings and sculptures, all of which served to give a glittering brilliance to often short-lived princes and dynasties. In later centuries, through miniatures, we have a much clearer vision of the delicately artificial world of courtly patronage, and for the very early centuries our information also is more adequate and leads to the same conclusions. Throughout the literature of Iran, in particular in poetical imagery and thematic inspiration, a sense of the primacy of a princely vocabulary of ideas and symbols is constantly present; and in more popular legends, such as in the Arabian Nights, it is again the same idealized world of caliphs and viziers which forms the backbone of the story and many of its details. While so many aspects of the Iranian world in the Middle Ages may thus appear as immersed in forms of princely inspiration, in the Jazirah or in Anatolia the same was true, although in slightly different terms. Iranian modes of life and thought were imitated there, and the superb quality of prosaic caravanseraglios may be explained as expressions of princely vanity as well as attempts to capture trade routes. As to the private foundations and mausoleums, their aristocratic character is almost always demonstrable in the inscriptions. It could then be argued that the monuments reflected the wealthy tastes of the princes and that the aim of the decoration was to transform sober pious buildings into glittering palaces. It was a world of Renaissance patrons rather than of medieval monks, and even if the avowed functions of the buildings often served the aims and purposes of the faith, their wealth of decoration was dictated by a secular ideal.

If our first point is to emphasize the princely aspect of so much of the architecture illustrated here — and thereby to explain the ubiquitous wealth of decoration — our second point may serve to explain the unbelievable variety of decorative themes and techniques. Their respective developments are not always closely connected, for the same themes were created in many techniques and certain regions preferred some techniques or themes to others. The underlying factor here seems to be that, in spite of the clear movements of people and ideas which took place from east to west, artistic techniques and themes were not simply those of Central Asia carried westward. In reality it is a wealth of ideas and forms from everywhere which appears. Traditional Iranian techniques, rude Armenian or Caucasian stone sculpture, Central Asian textile motifs, perhaps even nomadic themes from farther north (details on figs. 280, 474, 512–13 bear a strangely close resemblance to Celtic themes), Chinese scroll patterns, and many other elements occur in this decoration, because the architecture was produced by a world of movement and turmoil, in which artisans or objects from the whole Eurasian mass were available almost everywhere. Thus it is that an almost endless variety of themes — eventually to be explained region by region and period by period — can be understood in the light of the great ethnic, social, and economic migrations of the time.

As royal inspiration and taste gave it value and as the numbers of people involved brought it variety, the ornament of the time, within itself and in relationship to the architecture which used it, fully expressed the tensions of the complex culture which created it. And it is perhaps ultimately as the expression of this culture, so varied as to shirk definition, so wide as to lack unity, yet so unmistakably different from any of the cultures which were near it, or which followed and preceded it, that the ornament can best be understood. Except in a few of the more remarkable fifteenth-century monuments of the Timurids in Mashhad, Samarkand, and Herat, there are no perfect creations here, none of the great monuments which will characterize the age of the empires, when Ottomans, Safavids, and Mughals will erect the Suleymaniye, the *masjid-i shah* and the Taj Mahal. But these later achievements would hardly have been possible without the movements of men and ideas, and the development of themes and techniques which characterized the preceding period. It is in this sense that I have called this period classical, for it created a vocabulary of forms, purposes, and ideas which continued for several centuries as the major features of the architecture and ornament of an Islamic world which never recaptured the degree of unity it had in the early part of the thirteenth century. Just as no land ever occupied by Rome escaped the impact of Roman forms, so it is also that in the Near East no land which witnessed major artistic developments of the eleventh to thirteenth centuries ever abandoned their architectural and decorative lessons.

IV. BIBLIOGRAPHICAL NOTES

The purpose of these notes is merely to indicate the main works which have been used in preparing the introductory essay and to suggest further readings. No attempt has been made to achieve any kind of completeness.

1. *The historical and cultural setting.* Since there is no adequate history of the Islamic Near East, information has to be gathered either in the *Encyclopedia of Islam* or in specific monographs, of which the more important are: B. Spuler, *Iran in früh-islamischer Zeit* (Wiesbaden, 1952), and *Die Mongolen in Iran* (Berlin, 1955); W. Barthold, *Turkestan down to the Mongol Invasion* (2nd edition reprinted London, 1958); chapters by B. Lewis, H. A. R. Gibb, and especially C. Cahen in K. M. Setton and others, *A History of the Crusades*, 2 vols. published so far (Philadelphia, 1958 and 1962); numerous articles by C. Cahen mostly available now through J. D. Pearson, *Index Islamicus*, 1 vol. and suppl. (London, 1958 and 1962); V. Gordlevskij, *Gosudarstvo Seljukidov Maloi Azij* (Moscow, 1941); M. F. F. Köprülü, *Les origines de l'empire ottoman*, (Paris, 1935); P. Wittek, *The Rise of the Ottoman Empire* (London, 1958).

2. *The monuments.* For specific buildings the bibliography is indicated in the catalogue of monuments. There are no general studies pertaining specifically to the period and areas under consideration. A considerable amount of information can be gathered from the following volumes, although none is properly complete:

(*a*) Central Asia: G. A. Pugachenkova, *Puti Razvitiia Arhitektury Iuzhnogo Turkmenistana* (Moscow, 1958), particularly important because it deals with the area along the Persian frontier and with the city of Merv, not accessible to Westerners; G. A. Pugachenkova and L. I. Rempel, *Vydaiuchiesia Pamiatniki Arhitektury Uzbekistana* (Tashkent, 1958).

(*b*) Iran: A. U. Pope, ed., *A Survey of Persian Art* (London, 1939), rather uneven in the text; D. Wilber, *The Architecture of Islamic Iran, the Ilkhanid Period* (Princeton, 1955); A. Godard, *L'Art de l'Iran* (Paris, 1962); important articles by A. Godard, M. B. Smith, and others in *Athar-é Iran*, the *Bulletin of the American Association for Persian Art and Archaeology*, *Ars Islamica*, and *Ars Orientalis*.

(*c*) Jazirah: F. Sarre and E. Herzfeld, *Archäologische Reise im Tigris-und Euphratgebiet* (Berlin, 1911–20); W. Bachmann, *Kirchen und Moscheen in*

86

Armenien und Kurdistan (Leipzig, 1913); C. Preusser, *Nordmesopotamische Baudenkmäler* (Leipzig, 1911).

(*d*) Azerbayjan: A. Useinov, L. Bretanitskij, and others, *Istoriia Arhitektury Azerbayjana* (Moscow, 1963).

(*e*) Northern Syria: J. Sauvaget, *Alep* (Paris, 1941).

(*f*) Anatolia: the most convenient available surveys are by E. Diez and O. Aslanapa, *Türk Sanati* (Istanbul, 1955); T. Talbot Rice, *The Seljuks in Asia Minor* (London, 1961); S. K. Yetkin, *L'Architecture turque en Turquie* (Paris, 1962). A model of thorough research can be found in K. Erdmann, *Das Anatolische Karavanseray* (Berlin, 1962). Also, the two important works of A. Gabriel *Les Monuments Turcs d'Anatolie*, 2 vols. (1934) and *La Turquie Orientale*, 2 vols. (1940), both published by E de Boccard, Paris.

3. *Decoration and architecture*. The two principal studies on Central Asia are B. P. Denike, *Arhitekturnyi Ornament Srednei Azij* (Moscow, 1939) and L. I. Rempel, *Arhitekturnyi Ornament Uzbekistana* (Tashkent, 1961). On Iran a general survey exists in the *Survey of Persian Art* and an important article is that of D. N. Wilber, 'The Development of Mosaic Faience,' *Ars Islamica*, vol. VI (1939).

GLOSSARY

This glossary only includes those terms peculiar to Islamic history or archaeology which cannot be found in the usual dictionaries. For further information see *The Encyclopedia of Islam.*

AMIR: most common title for an administrative officer in early times, for any feudal or semi-feudal lord after the 10th century.

EYVAN: technically speaking, a large vaulted hall, with one side opening directly on the outside; often used to mean simply a covered hall in a mosque or in a palace; p. 52.

GHAZI: a complex term referring primarily to the militant spirit of the Holy War; of particular significance in the development of Turkic peoples within the Muslim world; p. 34.

IMAMZADEH: literally, 'the son of an *imam* (or leader of the community)'; in Iran usual term for a saint's mausoleum.

KHANGAH: Muslim equivalent of the monastery; p. 43.

MADRASAH: literally, 'school'; specifically, theological school for orthodoxy; pp. 42–3.

MIHRAB: niche in the mosque or in any religious building supposed to indicate the direction of prayer; but see p. 77.

MUQARNAS: original Islamic design involving various combinations of three-dimensional shapes; also called stalactite or honeycomb; p. 80.

MUSALLA: place for prayer, usually a wide open space outside the city; the history of the term is still uncertain; pp. 50–1.

PISHTAQ: technical Persian term for the monumental gateway; p. 78.

RIBAT: institution in which men gathered to live together in order to fight for the faith; pp. 34, 43.

SULTAN: originally the title of the principal civil and military leader of the Muslim world; later debased to include almost any prince.

1. BUKHARA. The Tomb of the Samanids, entrance. Tenth century

2. The Tomb of the Samanids (recently restored)

3. BUKHARA. Maghak-i Attari mosque, entrance. Early twelfth century

4. Maghak-i Attari mosque, detail of façade flanking entrance

5. Maghak-i Attari mosque, detail of entrance porch

6. Maghak-i Attari mosque, main entrance detail

7. (*above*) Maghak-i Attari mosque,
detail of façade

8. Maghak-i Attari mosque, detail
of façade

9. BUKHARA. Kalayan mosque, main dome seen from the bazaar. Early sixteenth century

10. (*below*) Minaret of the Kalayan mosque (so-called Tower of Death). A.D. 1127

11. Detail of Kalayan mosque minaret

12. Kalayan mosque, main courtyard—now being repaired

13. near BUKHARA. Vabkent, detail of minaret, A.D. 1198–9

14. (*below*) BUKHARA. Namazgah mosque, sixteenth century

15. BUKHARA. Mir-i Arab
madrasah, detail of archway in
main courtyard

16. Mir-i Arab *madrasah*,
main courtyard, being re-
stored. A.D. 1530–1536

17. BUKHARA.
Ulugh beg *madrasah*,
detail of tilework on
main entrance arch

18. Ulugh beg *madra-
sah*, *eyvan* arch in main
courtyard. A.D. 1417

19. BUKHARA. Abd al-Azia
khan *madrasah*, main entrance
—facing that of Ulugh beg *madrasah*. Mid-seventeenth century

20. (*below*) Abd al-Azia khan
madrasah, interior of courtyard

21. BUKHARA.
Madrasah of Abd Allah khan, main entrance. This portal faces the portal of the Madar-i Shah *madrasah*. Late sixteenth century

22. Abd Allah khan *madrasah*, detail of the main portal

23. Abd Allah khan *madrasah*, detail of courtyard showing entrance arch

24. BUKHARA. Madar-i Shah (Mother of the Shah) *madrasah*. Main entrance, late sixteenth century

25. BUKHARA. Char Bakr mosque, main courtyard. Mid-sixteenth century

26. Char Bakr mosque, detail of main dome

27. Char Bakr mosque, one of the main entrances

28. Char Bakr mosque, detail of tile lettering round the main door

29. BUKHARA. *Khangah* of Nadir Divan-beg, main *mihrab*. This building is now used as a club billiard room. Early seventeenth century

30. (*below*) BUKHARA. Detail of doorway to Buyan-Quly-khan mausoleum *ca*. A.D. 1359

31. SAMARKAND. Gur-i Amir, main facade and dome below which lies the Tomb of Tamerlane.
First half of the fifteenth century

32. Gur-i Amir, detail of dome and back of the tomb chamber exterior

33. (*below*) Gur-i Amir, detail of tile-work on entrance arch

34. Gur-i Amir. So-called throne of Tamerlane i marble, dug up in cour yard.

35. Gur-i Amir, tilewo on portal at main entrar to tomb

36. Gur-i Amir, tiled arches flanking main entrance to tomb

37 & 38. Gur-i Amir, two details of tilework on entrance arch

39. SAMARKAND. Bibi Khanum mosque, minaret at western corner of main *eyvan*. Early fifteenth century

40. Bibi Khanum mosque, main *eyvan* leading to holy hall of prayers begun A.D. 1399. Photographed by Count Morra in the 1890s

41. Bibi Khanum mosque, main entrance to the mosque. The central doorway is now destroyed and only a broken archway remains. Photographed by Count Morra in the 1890s

42. Minaret at the back of Bibi Khanum mosque

43. Corner minaret flanking main *eyvan* of Bibi Khanum mosque

44. Bibi Khanum mosque, minaret at eastern corner of main *eyvan*

45. (*above*) Bibi Khanum mosque, tilework on inside of damaged main entrance portal of mosque

46. Bibi Khanum mosque, detail of main entrance arch to the mosque

47. Bibi Khanum mosque, detail of arch over entrance to mosque, still intact in the 1890s (see fig. 41).

48. Further detail as above, of main entrance to mosque

49. Bibi Khanum
mosque, a detail of
arch flanking main
entrance to mosque

50. Bibi Khanum
mosque, tilework on
arch at main entrance

51. (*above*) Bibi Khanum mosque, base of dome at western side of main courtyard

52. Building at western side of main court of Bibi Khanum

53. Bibi Khanum mosque, detail of main *eyvan* arch leading to holy hall of prayer

54. Same as above, with dome above prayer hall showing through ruined façade

55. Detail of tiled lettering and pattern around dome of main prayer hall of Bibi Khanum mosque

56. Entrance to main prayer hall of Bibi Khanum mosque

57. Façade of main doorway to holy prayer hall, Bibi Khanum mosque

58. (*below*) Detail of eastern side of archway and façade leading to prayer hall of Bibi Khanum mosque

59. SAMARKAND.
Mausoleum of Ishrat
khaneh, detail of tile
and brickwork at rear
of building. A.D. 1464

60. SAMARKAND.
Registan   Square.
Ulugh beg *madrasah*,
main entrance, begun
A.D. 1420

61. Minaret and part of main entrance arch to Ulugh beg *madrasah*

62. Detail of tilework on main entrance to Ulugh beg *madrasah*

this page
63. (*above*) Detail of tilework on *eyvan* in interior courtyard of Ulugh beg *madrasah*

64. (*below*) Superb tilework on the main entrance arch to Ulugh beg *madrasah*

facing page
65. (*above*) SAMARKAND. Registan Square, showing Shir-dar *madrasah*. Early seventeenth century

66. (*below*) Shir-dar *madrasah* entrance. Both photographs taken by Count Morra in the 1890s

67. SAMARKAND. Tilework on tower at corner of Tilia-kari mosque and *madrasah* on the eastern side of Registan Square. Mid-seventeenth century

68. Mosque and courtyard of Tilia-kari

69. Detail of entrance to Tilia-kari mosque and *mad-rasah*

70. (*below*) Tower and main dome of Tilia-kari mosque

71. SAMARKAND. Shah-i Zindah ensemble of cemeteries, main view of whole. Photographed by Count Morra in the 1890s. Entrance A.D. 1454

72. Detail of Tuman aka mausoleum, Shah-i Zindah. A.D. 1405

73. Tilework at entrance to Tuman aka mausoleum

74. Mausoleum of Khoja Ahmad, entrance detail, Shah-i Zindah.
Fourteenth century

75. Khoja Ahmad mausoleum in Shah-i Zindah ensemble.
Photographed by Count Morra in the 1890s

76. Detail of tilework on so-called mausoleum of Ali, Shah-i Zindah

77. Exterior of so-called mausoleum of Ali, showing dome over tomb chamber, Shah-i Zindah

78. (*below*) Mausoleum of Ali, detail of exterior tile- and brickwork. Fourteenth century

79. Very elaborate tilework at entrance to tomb of Shad-i Mulk Aka. A.D. 1372. Shah-i Zindah

80. Mausoleum of Tuglu-Tekin, arch at entrance to tomb chamber. A.D. 1372. Shah-i Zindah

81. Entrance to mauso-
leum of Emir Zadah.
A.D. 1386. Shah-i Zin-
dah

82. Entrance to mausoleum of
Emir Zadah and, in foreground,
part of façade to the adjoining
mausoleum of Shad-i Mulk Aka

83. (*above*) Shah-i Zindah. Detail of tilework on inside of arch leading to mausoleum of Ulugh-Sultan Begim. Fourteenth century

84. Façade of arch leading to mausoleum of Ulugh-Sultan Begim. Shah-i Zindah

85. Unidentified mausoleum in Shah-i Zindah ensemble. Photographed by Count Morra in the
1890s. Dated A.D. 1360–61

86. Shah-i Zindah. Unidentified mausoleum (detail). A.D. 1360–61

87. (*above*) Shah-i Zin-
dah, tilework on ex-
terior of unidentified
mausoleum

88. Detail of angle in
entrance to unidentified
mausoleum.   Shah-i
Zindah

89. Shah-i Zindah. Mausoleum of Kaz-Zadah-Rum. Fifteenth century

90. SAMARKAND. Mazar of Khoja Abd-i Birun, detail of dome and façade. 1633

91. SHAHR-I SABZ. Tilework in interior of arched gateway at Tamerlane's palace

92. Another detail of above

93. SHAHR-I SABZ. Tiles, lettering and brickwork on the tower part of the Akserai palace

94. One of the stumps of the
great arch of Tamerlane's palace
in Akserai. Begun at turn of
fourteenth and fifteenth century

95. Detail of tilework on interior of ruined 'stump'

96. Further detail of tile-work on interior wall of Akserai

97. Walls in interior of palace

98. Tilework on inside of entrance arch of palace at Shahr-i Sabz

99. Stucco work of later date, copying fourteenth-century design in brickwork at Shahr-i Sabz

100. SHAHR-I SABZ.
Mausoleum of Jehangir, late
fourteenth century

101. The interior section
of above mausoleum

102. SHAHR-I SABZ. Gunbadh-i Sayyidan

103. SHAHR-I SABZ. Kok Gunbadh under repair

104. TURKESTAN. Exterior of Khoja Ahmad Yassavi 'complex'. A.D. 1397

105. Different angle of above

106. Mausoleum entrance to the 'complex' that contains a mosque, mausoleum, *khangah* and library

107. Main entrance to the Khoja Ahmad Yassavi 'complex'

108. Side view of 'complex' in Turkestan

109. Arrival entrance of above

110. Entrance of mausoleum in the Khoja Ahmad Yassavi 'complex'

111. Detail of dome over the mausoleum, Khoja Ahmad Yassavi 'complex'

112. (*above*) UZGEND.
Mausoleum of Jelal al-din
al-Husayn. A.D. 1152

113. Detail of tilework on
entrance arch of above
mausoleum

114. UZGEND. Detail of entrance porch of middle mausoleum A.D. 1187

115. Inside arch at entrance to mausoleum shown above

116. A further detail of tilework
on the same mausoleum

117. Detail of above
pillar

118. Further detail of same entrance
porch façade

119. Another detail showing
patterned brickwork

120. URGENCH. Entrance of mausoleum known as Turabek khanum. Early fourteenth century

121. URGENCH. Mausoleum of Tekesh. Early thirteenth century

122. URGENCH. The earliest mausoleum at Urgench, supposedly of Fakhr al-din Ghazi. *ca.* A.D. 1208

123. TIRMIDH. Mausoleum of Husayn, interior. Part of Sultan Saadet ensemble, eleventh or twelfth century

124. (*above*) GHUJDAWAN.
Ulugh beg *madrasah* entrance.
A.D. 1433

125. Minaret near entrance

AFGHANISTAN

126. HERAT.
Mausoleum of Gawhar
Shad, exterior. Fifteenth
century

127. Dome of above
and side wall

128 & 129. Interior photographs of Gawhar Shad's mausoleum, both taken by Josephine Powell

130. HERAT. Interlacing archways in the main (congregational) mosque. Probably twelfth century

131. HERAT. Exterior of *masjid-i* Jami. Timurid tilework over an earlier
Seljuq archway

132. Same as above showing a further detail of later Timurid work over earlier Seljuq decoration

133. (*below*) HERAT. The now only remaining minaret forming part of Gawhar Shad's *madrasah* or *musalla*. Photograph by Josephine Powell

134. (*right*) HERAT. Two of the corner minarets belonging to the destroyed Husayn Bayqara *madrasah*. A.D. 1469–1506

135. (*above*) the four remaining minarets of the Husayn Bayqara *madrasah*

136. HERAT. Lettering in tiles and patterning on the old walls of the town. Early fifteenth century

137. HERAT. Gazur Gah. Tile decoration in sanctuary of Khwajah Abd allah Ansari. A.D. 1428–29

138. Further detail of decoration at the entrance to the sanctuary

139. Gazur-Gah, tilework in prayer hall of Abd allah Ansari shrine

140. The lower section of the above wall showing tile-work

141. (*above*) Gazur Gah. Carved marble side of sarcophagus in courtyard

142. Tilework on side prayer chamber at Gazur Gah shrine

143. CHIST. Tomb o
a khwajah. Photograph
by Reinhard Schlagint
weit. Probably late
twelfth century

144. CHIST.
Ruined remains of
another mausoleum.
Photograph by
Reinhard Schlagint-
weit

145. GHAZNI. Tower of victory with name of Mas‘ud III. A.D. 1089–1115

149. GHAZNI. Upper portion of so-called tower of Mahmud, built in fact for the
Ghaznevid Prince Bahramshah. A.D. 1117–1149

150. Detail of preceding tower. Photograph by Josephine Powell

151. JAM. The minaret of Jam. A.D. 1153–1203

152. (*above*) BUST. Qal'ah-i Bust, arch recently restored. Probably twelfth century

153. Detail of decoration on inside of arch

154. Detail of Qal‘ah-i Bust arch

155. Mausoleum at Qal'ah-i Bust called Giyath al-din. Eleventh or twelfth century

156. Another view of above mausoleum

157. Detail of arch on mausoleum at Qal'ah-i Bust

158. Interior of the mausoleum showing patterned brickwork

159. Detail of decorative under-arch on mausoleum

160. Another detail of above arch

161. BUST. Ruins of the Ghaznevid palace of Lashkari Bazar

162. Detail of an entrance to the palace

163. BALKH.
Archway to shrine
of Khwajah Akash,
late fourteenth cen-
tury

164. BALKH. De-
tail of decorative
tilework on shrine
of Khwajah Abu
Nasr Parsa. A.D.
1460–1

165. Another detail of tilework at shrine of Khwajah Abu Nasr Parsa

166. Further detail of above. All photographs of Balkh were taken by Josephine Powell

167. near BALKH. Minaret of Dawlatabad. A.D. 1108–9

168. Detail of minaret of Dawlatabad. Both photographs by Josephine Powell

169. SANGBAST. Detail of roof brickwork at mausoleum of Arslan Jadhib. A.D. 1028

170. Detail of squinch and painted frieze of Kufic lettering inside mausoleum of Arslan Jadhib

171. TAYABAD. Tilework in prayer *eyvan* at shrine of Zayn al-din. Early fifteenth century

172. Another detail of tilework in the same *eyvan*

173. Tilework on façade
of Zayn al-din shrine

174. (*above*) Shrine of Zayn al-din courtyard

175. TURBAT-I SHAYKH-JAM.
Entrance arch to mausoleum of Ahmad
al-Hasan. Fifteenth century

176. GUNBADH-I QABUS.
The mausoleum tower of a
prince. A.D. 1007

177. (*below*) Detail of above,
showing Kufic lettering in brick.

178. (*above*)
HAMADAN.
Gunbadh-i Alaviyan,
main façade. Probably
twelfth century

179. Detail of above
façade

180. Stucco decoration over doorway to Gunbadh-i Alaviyan

181. (*below*) Another detail of the façade of the mausoleum

this page
182. (*above*) Stucco decoration in interior of mausoleum

183. (*below*) Another detail of the above mausoleum

facing page
184. (*top left*) BISTAM. Minaret of shrine called al-Bistam. *ca.* A.D. 1120

185. (*top right*) Entrance to shrine. Most of the shrine datable A.D. 1300

186. (*below*) The archway roof at approach to saint's shrine

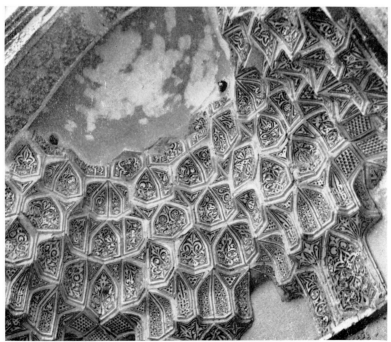

187. Detail of decoration inside arch

188. Another detail of decoration and tilework in the archway

189. BISTAM. *Mihrab* in the mosque of Bayazid al-Bistami shrine

190. Detail of stucco work at side of *mihrab*

191. Detail of wall
in the shrine mosque

192. Kufic lettering
on *mihrab* wall in
the shrine mosque

193. Detail of top of
tomb tower showing
Kufic inscriptions.
Probably twelfth
century

194. BISTAM. Tomb
tower attached to the
shrine mosque

195. Detail of brickwork on the tomb tower

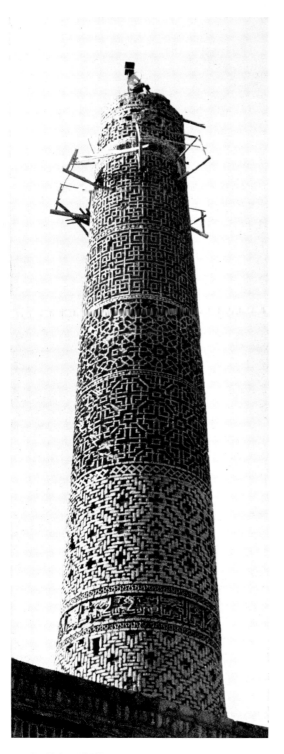

196. DAMGHAN. Tarik-khaneh minaret. Early eleventh century

197. DAMGHAN. Main mosque minaret. *ca.* A.D. 1058

198. (*above*)
DAMGHAN. Mausoleum of Pir-i 'Alamdar.
A.D. 1027

199. DAMGHAN.
Detail of roof of Chihil Dukhteran mausoleum, showing Kufic lettering on brickwork.
A.D. 1056

200. DAMGHAN. Interior of Tarik-khaneh, the oldest mosque in Iran in its original condition. Eighth or ninth century

201. YAZD. Main prayer *eyvan* of Cheqmaq mosque. A.D. 1436

202. (*above*)
YAZD. Detail of
portal of Abu
al-Qasim mosque.
Fourteenth century

203. A further de-
tail of above doorway

204. YAZD. Detail of tilework at
main entrance to *masjid-i* Jum'ah.
Mid-fourteenth century

205. (*below*) Interior of prayer
chamber in *masjid-i* Jum'ah

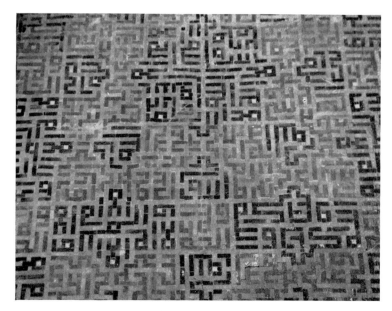

206. Further tilework in *masjid-i* Jum'ah mosque

207. YAZD. Tilework and hollyhocks in the courtyard of the Shams al-din 'mausoleum' courtyard. *ca.* A.D. 1365. Photograph by John Creighton

208. Tilework at the entrance to the Shams al-din *madrasah*. Mid-fourteenth century

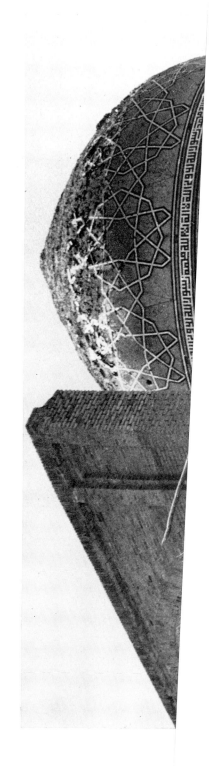

216. TABRIZ. Detail of tile-work in so-called Blue Mosque

217. (*below*) Entrance to 'Blue Mosque', now being restored. A.D. 1465

218. (*above*) Tilework in main courtyard of 'Blue Mosque'. A.D. 1465

219. TABRIZ. Walls of mosque of 'Ali Shah (so-called the Ark). *ca.* A.D. 1310–20

220. Detail of brickwork on 'Ali Shah mosque walls

221. MARAGHAH. Entrance to Gunbadh-i Ghaffariyah. A.D. 1316

222. Gunbadh-i Ghaffariyah

223. (*above*) MARAGHAH. Gunbadh-i
Surkh. A.D. 1147

224. MARAGHAH. Carved inscription in
lower chamber of Gunbadh-i Kabud. A.D.
1196–7

225. (*above*) Gunbadh-i Kabud

226. MARAGHAH. Gunbadh Joi Burj. *ca.* A.D. 1330

227. NAKHICHEVAN. Mausoleum of Yusuf b. Kathir. A.D. 1161–2

228. Detail of the doorway

229. NAKHICHEVAN. Mausoleum of Mu'minah Khatun. Part of the façade. A.D. 1186–7

230. KARABAGLAR. Fourteenth century mausoleum, detail of entrance

231 & 232. JUGA. Thirteenth
century mausoleum (unidentified)
and details of its façade

233. BARDA. Mausoleum dated
A.D. 1322

234. Detail of mausoleum entrance

235. SULTANIYAH. The mausoleum of Oljaytu. One of the finest Islamic buildings in Asia and in desperate need of restoration before the dome collapses. A.D. 1307–1313

236. (*above*) The dome of
the mausoleum rising above
the village roofs

237. The interior of the
Oljaytu mausoleum

238. Details of roof tiling in the galleries around the dome of the Oljaytu mausoleum

239. Another detail as above

240. A further roof detail

241. Part of the exterior dome gallery of the mausoleum

242. Tilework on exterior of Oljaytu mausoleum

243. Another detail of above

244. Stucco work,
formerly enclosed,
from ruined prayer
chamber of Oljaytu
mausoleum

245. Archway with
tilework over an en-
trance to the Oljaytu
mausoleum

246. Another entrance to the Oljaytu mausoleum showing tilework around the archway

247. (*below*) SULTANIYAH. Tomb of Mullah Hasan, detail of tilework and arch. Sixteenth century

248. SULTANIYAH. Tilework on wall and archway, mausoleum of Oljaytu

249. SULTANIYAH. Tomb of Chelebi Oglu. Patterned brickwork above a stone base. *ca.* A.D. 1330

250. QAZVIN.
Mihrab in main
prayer chamber (being
restored) of the con-
gregational mosque.
Twelfth century

251. Dome of congrega-
tional mosque above main
prayer chamber. A.D. 1113

252. (above) RAYY. Detail
of unknown tomb tower.
Probably early twelfth century

253. VERAMIN. *Imamza-
deh* of Shah Husayn, *mihrab*
in interior of mausoleum.
Probably fourteenth century.
Photograph by Jeremy Fry

254. VERAMIN. Tomb of Ala al-din. A.D. 1289

255. (below) Detail of roof section of Ala al-din mausoleum

256. (*above left*) VERAMIN. Detail of interior of main prayer *eyvan* of congregational mosque

257. (*above right*) Tilework on entrance archway to congregational mosque

258. Arches in covered arcade surrounding the main courtyard of congregational mosque

259. Brick and stucco decoration under archway in interior of congregational mosque

260. Detail of corner wall of gateway of congregational mosque

261. Detail of wall and roofing of main prayer *eyvan* of congregational mosque

262. Another detail of above

263. *Mihrab* in main prayer chamber of congregational mosque

264. NATANZ. Entrance to the *khangah*, being restored. A.D. 1316–17

265. Decorative lettering and pattern used at the entrance to the *khangah*

266. Façade of *khangah* being restored

267. Detail of tile
work above a niche
inside entrance arch
to *khangah*

268. Another detail
of the niche

269. Tilework on en-
trance archway to *khan-
gah*

270. Exterior of Natanz *khangah* showing the wall below
the minaret

271. NATANZ. *Khangah* minaret and dome over tomb. Between A.D. 1304 and 1325

272. NATANZ. Detail of Kufic inscription on inside of archway of congregational mosque

273. ARDISTAN.
Archway and decoration in congregational
mosque

274. Decorative
feature and brick-
work in interior of
congregational
mosque

275. Stucco work super-imposed over brick on interior *eyvan* of congregational mosque

276. Ruined archways with painted decoration, congregational mosque

277. NAYIN. Early stucco work over an
arch in the main mosque. Tenth century

278. Pillar in the main
mosque. Tenth century

281. GULPAYGAN.
Brick- and tilework and
Kufic lettering beside
the *mihrab* in the con-
gregational mosque.
Early twelfth century

282. (*below*) Detail of
wall in main prayer
eyvan of congregational
mosque

285 & 284. Two details of decorative Kufic lettering around the *mihrab* of congregational mosque

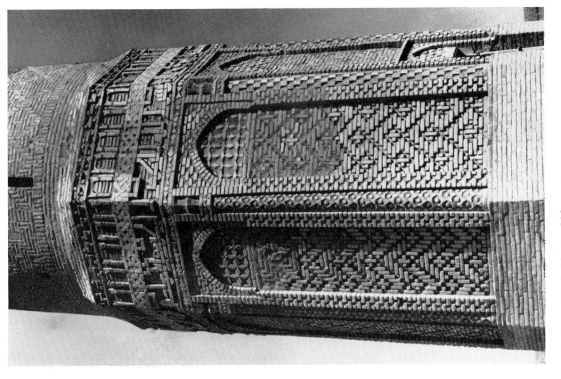

285 & 286. GULPAYGAN. Minaret in the town. Probably twelfth century

287. LINJAN. Pir-i Baq-
ran sanctuary. A.D. 1299–1311

288. Ceiling decoration in the
sanctuary shrine

289. Stucco decoration above a niche in the sanctuary shrine

290. Pir-i Baqran, extremely rich stucco decoration in the *mihrab*

291. Sanctuary wall decoration, Pir-i Baqran

292. Opposite wall to the above in the shrine

293. Decorative stucco on an angle wall of the shrine

294. (*below*) Detail of *mihrab* stucco decoration of Pir-i Baqran sanctuary

295. The entrance to Pir-i Baqran sanctuary at Linjan. Use of Kufic lettering as ornament on brickwork

296. ASHTARJAN. Roof
to the entrance arch of the
village mosque, recently
restored. *ca.* A.D. 1315

297. Variety of tile- and
brickwork in the mosque
entrance portal

298. Decoration in stucco and brick on arch and roof of village mosque

299. Another window arch and its decoration at the village mosque

300. Detail of wall decoration of the mosque

301. Turquoise blue tile calligraphy as ornament in the mosque

this page
302. (*above*) Detail of *mihrab* in the village mosque

303. (*below*) The *mihrab* with stucco decoration in the mosque

facing page
304 & 305. ISFAHAN. The congregational (Friday) mosque. Two *eyvans* in the main mosque courtyard. Twelfth century with later decoration added

306. *Mihrab* in the congregational (Friday) mosque. Ordered by the Ilkhanid Oljaytu who was buried at Sultaniyah. Dated A.D. 1310. Photograph by D. Hicks

307. The congregational (Friday) mosque, detail of wall lining the northern (small) dome chamber

308. A *mihrab* dated A.D. 1308 to compare with fig. 306. Now in the Teheran museum, this mihrab was formerly in the Rabi 'ah Khatun sanctuary at Ashtarjan.

309. ISFAHAN. Another detail of wall in the congregational mosque

310. Wall decoration with use of Kufic in congregational mosque. Fourteenth or fifteenth century

311. Further wall decoration in same prayer *eyvan* as above

312. (*above*) ISFAHAN.
Entrance to former Jorjir
mosque. Deylamite work,
tenth century

313. ISFAHAN. Do Minar
Dardasht tomb chamber en-
trance, archway detail. A.D.
1330–40

515. ISFAHAN. Do Minar Dardasht entrance archway

514. ISFAHAN. Base of Bagh-i Qush khaneh minaret. Fourteenth century

517. ISFAHAN. Chihil Dukhtaran minaret base. A.D. 1107

516. ISFAHAN. *Masjid* Ali minaret. Probably late twelfth century

318. ISFAHAN. Bagh-i Qush
khaneh minaret. Fourteenth century

319. ISFAHAN. Saraban (or camel
driver's) minaret. Fourteenth century

520. MASHHAD. Gawhar Shad mosque, courtyard and northern prayer *eyvan*. Completed
A.D. 1405–6

321. Tilework on arch leading to main prayer chamber of Gawhar Shad mosque

322. MASHHAD. Painted
decoration below dome (tem-
porarily under repair) of main
prayer chamber in Gawhar
Shad mosque

323. *Mihrab* in main prayer
chamber (under repair) of
Gawhar Shad mosque

324. MASHHAD. Minaret above main prayer chamber of Gawhar Shad mosque

325. Base of dome on Gawhar Shad mosque

326. MASHHAD. Base of minaret in courtyard of congregational mosque. Fifteenth century

327. (*below*) TUS. Mausoleum known as Haruniyah. Date as yet uncertain, possibly early twelfth century

TURKEY

328. ERZERUM. General view of city

329. E R Z E R U M. Mausoleum
behind the Cifte Minareli *mad-*
rasah. Late twelfth or thirteenth
century

330. E R Z E R U M. Detail of
carved stonework inside courtyard
of Cifte Minareli *madrasah*. A.D.
1253.

331. (*above*) Main entrance to the Cifte
Minareli *madrasah*. A.D. 1253

332. Carved decorated pillars in courtyard of *madrasah*

333. Carved stone decoration in
Cifte Minareli *madrasah*

334. Courtyard of the *madra-sah*, showing the Cifte (twin)
minarets

335. Carved stonework at main entrance to Cifte Minareli *madrasah*

336. ERZERUM. Minaret in citadel, brickwork of thirteenth century, but summit of wood, probably nineteenth century

337. ERZERUM. Two unidentified tombs behind the *madrasah*

338. ERZERUM. Tomb behind the Yakutiye *madrasah*. These tombs are probably all thirteenth century

339. ERZERUM. Entrance to the Yakutiye *madrasah*, now used as a military store. *ca.* A.D. 1310

340. Courtyard of Yakutiye *madrasah*, showing entrance and stump of minaret

341. Detail of minaret of Yakutiye *madrasah* in turquoise tiles and red brickwork. *ca.* A.D. 1310

342. TERCAN. Mama Hatun türbesi, detail of actual tomb chamber exterior. *ca.* A.D. 1200

343. (*below*) Interior of courtyard of türbesi

344. Roof of tomb chamber of türbesi

345. *Muqarnas* or stalactite stone carving on the niche above entrance to türbesi

346. Entrance to the Mama Hatun türbesi

347. Detail of carved stonework at side of entrance to Mama Hatun

348. (*above*) Carving around entrance to türbesi

349. POZAR. Entrance to the caravanseraglio Hatun Han. A.D. 1238–9

350. Detail of over-arch in interior courtyard of caravan-seraglio

351. Detail of side of entrance to Hatun Han showing carved stone motif

352. (*above*) AMASYA.
Carved stone façade of the Halifet Gazi türbesi. A.D. 1142–6

353. AMASYA. Base of minaret at entrance to Burmali
Minare mosque. A.D. 1243

354. *(above)* A M A S Y A . Brick
and turquoise blue tile tower
to tomb above a mosque. Thirteenth century

355. A M A S Y A .　Turumtay
türbesi, detail of stone carving
on outside. A.D. 1278–9

356. AMASYA.
Bimarhane *madrasah*, detail of carved stone at window now blocked up. A.D. 1309

357. Main gateway to Bimarhane *madrasah* showing carved details

358. Niche inside the main entrance gateway to the Bimarhane

359. Niche opposite the
one above in main en-
trance

360. (*above*) TOKAT.
Detail of glazed tilework
on Gök *madrasah* interior
archway. A.D. 1295

361. Another detail as
above

362. TOKAT. Tomb of Nur
al-din b. Sentimur. A.D. 1314

363. NIKSAR. Brick pat-
terning above the entrance
to the Kirk Kizlar türbesi.
Early thirteenth century

364. SIVAS. So-called Güdük Minare or mausoleum of Sheikh Hasan Beyr. A.D. 1347–8

365. (*above*) SIVAS. Muzaffer Bürüciye *madrasah*, detail of carved stonework. Photograph by the Earl of Crawford

366. SIVAS. Blocked up archway. Detail of the entrance façade of the Cifte Minareli *madrasah*. Photograph by the Earl of Crawford

568. Gök *madrasah*, entrance, A.D. 1271-2

567. Entrance to Cifte Minareli *madrasah*. A.D. 1272. Photograph by the Earl of Crawford

570. Detail of carved stone pillar on entrance façade of *madrasah*

569. Detail of façade of Çifte Minareli *madrasah*. Photograph by the Earl of Crawford

371. Detail of pillar flanking main entrance to the *madrasah*

372. SIVAS. Muzaffer Bürüciye *madrasah*. Carved Kufic calligraphy ornamenting an interior archway. A.D. 1271–2

373. SIVAS. The hospital of Kai-kavus. Exterior of the King's tomb, decorated in blue tilework and red bricks

374. (*below*) Detail of the tower above the tomb of Kai-kavus. A.D. 1217

375. VAN. Unidentified thirteenth century tomb in the old city, now destroyed

376. BITLIS. Detail of decoration on main mosque. Possibly Ottoman

377. MALATYA. Main gateway and part of the minaret of the Great Mosque in Eski (or old) Malatya. Mid-thirteenth century

378. Interior of main courtyard of the Great Mosque showing tilework on the *eyvan* arch

379. Detail of brick- and tilework in the Great Mosque. Mid-thirteenth century

380. Unidentified stone column decorated with animal designs and lettering. Main courtyard of the Great Mosque

381. AK HAN. Main gateway. A.D. 1253–4

382. Detail of decoration on the main gateway to the Han. Both photographs taken by the Earl of Crawford

383. DIYARBAKR. The Great
Mosque courtyard. Façade of building on the north side. Partly twelfth
century with earlier columns

384. Detail of façade of
above building

385. (*above*) Kufic writing and
animal carving above the main
entrance archway to the Great
Mosque. Twelfth century

386. HOSAB (Van province).
Gateway to the castle, built into
the rock. Probably thirteenth
century

387 & 388. Two views of the great bridge over the Batman Su near Silvan. Dated A.D. 1146–7

389. Seljuq Bridge near Horosan. Photograph by Rear Admiral Paul Furse

390. Remains of Seljuq Bridge near Bayburt on the Trebizond-Erzerum road

391. (*above*) Two mausoleums
near Lake Van. On the left the
Bughatay Ata Türbe. A.D. 1281
and 1279

392. AHLAT. Mausoleum of
Erzen hatun. A.D. 1396–7

393. AHLAT. Detail of Bayindir
tomb. A.D. 1491

394. Unidentified tomb
at Ahlat

395. AHLAT. Ulu tomb, standing above the shores of Lake Van. A.D. 1273–81

396. (*above*)
MARDIN. Façade of
the Sultan Isa *madra-
sah* below the town
citadel. A.D. 1385

397. Main entrance to
the Sultan Isa *madra-
sah*

398. Detail of decoration at side of main entrance to Sultan Isa *madrasah*

399. Sultan Isa *madrasah*.
Interior of prayer chamber

400. (*above*) MARDIN. Window of courtyard of Şehidiye *madrasah*. Thirteenth century decoration

401. Kufic lettering, plant life and carving on courtyard wall of the Şehidiye *madrasah*

402. (*above*) MARDIN. Sultan Hamzah mausoleum outside the town

403. MARDIN. The Great Mosque. Kufic lettering at the base of the minaret. Late twelfth century

404. The Great Mosque minaret. *ca.* A.D. 1176

405. NISIBIN. Bricked-in arch showing 'flowering stone' decoration. Courtyard in front of the church of St James. Date uncertain

406. DOGAN BAYAZIT. Carving on a mock Seljuq eighteenth century
castle wall

407. KARS. Niche in a now disused mosque

408 & 409.
TREBIZOND. Seljuq type of decoration incorporated into the walls of the Church of Hagia Sophia

410. KONYA. Ince minaret and *madrasah*. A.D. 1258

411. Detail of the main entrance to Ince minaret *madrasah*

412. Rare animal carving of Seljuq period preserved in the interior of Ince minaret *madrasah*

413. One of the 'angels' formerly guarding the main gate to the city of Konya (now destroyed) preserved in the Ince minaret *madrasah*

414. KONYA. Alaeddin mosque, tomb in interior courtyard. The Alaeddin mosque is dated between A.D. 1155 and 1220

415. Window at rear of Alaeddin mosque

416. KONYA. Doorway of tomb in the compound of the Alaeddin mosque

417. KONYA. *Mihrab* in interior of mausoleum behind the Alaeddin mosque

418 & 419. Alaeddin mosque. A pair of carved
Seljuq wooden windows in the mosque

420. K O N Y A. Karatay *madrasah*, A.D. 1251. Main gateway. Pair of carved wooden doors preserved in interior

421. Tiled ceiling of the *madrasah*

422. Doors from Sufas mosque at Ermenak preserved in Karatay *madrasah*

423. (*below*) MERAM, near Konya. Blocked-in window of the old bath house. Possibly Ottoman

424. KONYA.
Decoration in a porch
at the Mevlana. The
carved stone above
the later door is Seljuq

425. KONYA. The Dar al-
Huffuz. A detail of the façade
dating from the Karamanli
period. Early fifteenth century

426. KONYA. Sircali *madrasah*, A.D. 1242. Detail of the carved main entrance porch

427. Sircali *madrasah*, tilework on façade of main *eyvan*

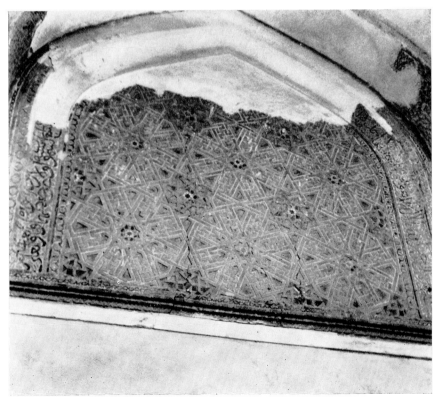

428. Tilework inside the *eyvan* of Sircali *madrasah*

429. KONYA. Sa'd al-din Han (outside Konya). Main entrance to the *han* or caravanseraglio. A.D. 1235–6

430. (*below*) Classical stones introduced into the outside walls of the Sa'd al-din Han.

431. Another wall of the Sa'd al-din Han with classical and early Christian tomb stones introduced

432. (*below*) Southern wall and great gateway of the Sa'd al-din Han

433. KONYA. Sahip Ata mausoleum, detail of tilework in tomb chamber. A.D. 1282

434. (below) KONYA. Sahip Ata mosque, detail of the work around the *mihrab*. A.D. 1279

435. Sahip Ata mosque. Detail of Seljuq wood carving on the door of the mosque. Mosque dated A.D. 1279

436. Sahip Ata mosque gateway, detail of façade

437. (*above*) KARAMAN. Imaret
of Ibrahim bey. A.D. 1426–62

438. Gateway, now blocked, at
side of imaret of Ibrahim bey

439. Detail of Ibrahim
bey imaret gateway

440. KARAMAN.
Detail of wall flanking
entrance to Hatuniye
madrasah

441. (*above*) Detail of
marble carving above
the main entrance to
Hatuniye *madrasah*.
A.D. 1382

442. Carving over an
interior doorway,
Hatuniye *madrasah*

443. KARAMAN. Entrance to a *madrasah* now used as a school

444. KARAMAN. Niche in main entrance to the Hatuniye *madrasah*

445. Hatuniye *madrasah*, detail of interior doorway

446. (*below*) Carved marble façade detail to main entrance of Hatuniye *madrasah*

447. KARAMAN. Detail of blocked window of Kizlar tomb

448. Kizlar tomb, outside the town. Mid-fifteenth century

449. Kizlar tomb, entrance

450. (*below*) BEYŞEHIR. Carved over-window of the Eşrefoglu mosque. A.D. 1298

451. Eşrefoglu mosque, carved wooden
Seljuq window shutter

452. (*below*) Eşrefoglu mosque. Detail
of tiled ceiling of the mausoleum of
Eşref Rum beside the mosque. *ca.* A.D.
1298

453. NIĞDE. Main entrance portal to the Alaeddin mosque. A.D. 1224

454. Detail of the Alaeddin mosque entrance façade

455. NIĞDE. Sunghur bey
mosque, 'rose' window and
doorway at side of the
mosque. A.D. 1338

456. Detail of original
carved wooden door to the
Sunghur bey mosque

457. NIĞDE. Khudavand tomb with side entrance. A.D. 1312

458. Main entrance to the Khudavand tomb

459. NIĞDE. Interior of the Ak *madrasah* courtyard, being repaired. A.D. 1409

460. Entrance, on the street, to Ak *madrasah*. Detail of carving over the porch

461. A K S E R A I. Sultan Han, carved marble façade at main entrance to the Han. A.D. 1229–79

462. (*above*) Courtyard of the Sultan Han, the
ruined edicule in the centre now being restored

463. AKSERAI. Unnamed minaret of Seljuq
origin in the town

464. SILVAN. *Mihrab* in the interior of the great mosque. *ca*. A.D. 1250

465. (*below*) SILVAN. Minaret outside the city walls. Probably thirteenth century

466. AGZIKARA HAN. The small mosque or edicule in the centre of the Han. A.D. 1236–46

467. Interior court-
yard and entrance to
the Han proper

468. Agzikara Han,
detail of entrance
from the road

469. Agzikara Han, courtyard from the roof

470. (*below*) KAYSERI. Sultan Han, interior entrance façade. A.D. 1232–6. Photograph by Josephine Powell

471. Detail of porch interior, entrance façade

472. Sultan Han, niche in main exterior entrance porch

473 & 474. Sultan Han, edicule in the main courtyard and a detail of its ornamentation. Both photographs by Josephine Powell

475. Sultan Han. Looking up from the caravanseraglio to the 'dome'

476. Detail of decoration around 'dome' in the centre of the caravanseraglio. Photograph by Josephine Powell

477. KAYSERI. Ali Ja'far tomb. A.D. 1247–8

478. KAYSERI.
Entrance to the Cifte
madrasah. A.D. 1206

479. KAYSERI.
The Huand Hatun
tomb. A.D. 1257–8

480. KAYSERI.
Madrasah of Hadji Kilidj,
main entrance A.D. 1275

481. KAYSERI. Cifte mausoleum. *ca*. A.D.
1270

482. KAYSERI. Detail of carving on the Huand Hatun tomb

483. Huand Hatun *madrasah*, western entrance

484. Eastern entrance

485. KAYSERI. Döner mausoleum. A.D. 1296

486. KAYSERI. Entrance to the Sahibiye *madrasah*. A.D. 1268

487. KARATAY
HAN. Main en-
trance to the Han.
A.D. 1230–40

488. Detail of main en-
trance porch, being re-
stored

489. (*above*) Courtyard and entrance to the caravanseraglio

490. Detail of the caravanseraglio entrance

491. Decoration on a blocked-up interior doorway

492. Decoration inside the main entrance arch to the Han

493. Section of the outside wall of the Han

494. Façade of a court-yard wall with the main entrance to the Han

495. (*above*) DIVRIG. The
Sitte Melik Türbe. A.D. 1196

496. DIVRIG. Entrance to
the hospital attached to the
Ulu Cami. The actual doorway
is of course modern

497. DIVRIG. Ulu Cami, main entrance portal to the mosque. A.D. *ca.* 1240

498. Seljuq two-headed eagles carved on the Ulu Cami wall

499. DIVRIG. Detail of entrance to the castle mosque

500. Eastern façade entrance to the Ulu Cami

501. (*below*) Entrance to the castle mosque

502. (*above*) ERCIS (Lake Van) Türbe near the Patnos road. Probably thirteenth century

503. Detail of the Türbe entrance

504. Detail of Türbe near the Patnos road

505. (*below*) Alay Han on Akserai-Urgup road. Main entrance to the Han. Probably late twelfth or early thirteenth century

506. GEVAS. Unidentified mausoleum near the shores of Lake Van

507. near AVAMOS. Sari Han. Gateway to the Han

508. Sari Han, niche in main entrance portal

509. near ANTALYA. Evdir Han. Main entrance to the Han. All
photographs (507 to 509) by Dr. Erdmer

510. DUNAYSIR. *Mihrab* in the mosque dated A.D. 1200

511. (*below*) Detail of the *mihrab*

512 & 515. DUNAYSIR. Doorways to the mosque. A.D. 1200

514. HISN-KAYFR. Tomb of Zaynal Beg. Mid-fifteenth century

SYRIA

515. ALEPPO. Detail of *eyvan* in the al-Firdaws *madrasah*

516. ALEPPO. Entrance to the Zahiriyah *madrasah*

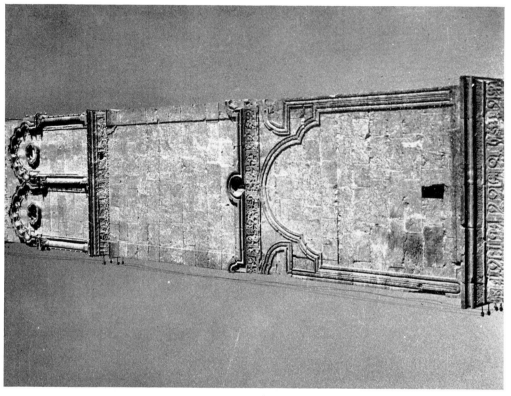

518. ALEPPO. Minaret of the congregational mosque. Eleventh century

517. ALEPPO. *Mihrab* in the Zahiriyah *madrasah*

519. ALEPPO. Part of the citadel walls and entrance. Twelfth and thirteenth centuries

520. Frontal view to main entrance of the citadel

521. ALEPPO. Courtyard
of the al-Firdaws *madrasah*

522. (*below left*) ALEPPO.
Façade at side of main entrance to the al-Utrush
mosque

523. (*below right*) The entrance to the al-Utrush
mosque. A.D. 1403

INDIA

524. DELHI. The Qutb minaret. A.D. 1206. Both photographs by Roderick Cameron

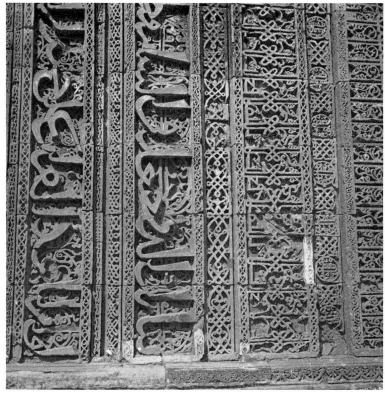

525. AJMIR. *Arhai-din-ka-Jhompra*. Detail of façade beside the main entrance. *ca.* A.D. 1200

526. *Arhai-din-ka-Jhompra,*
detail of archway. Photo-
graph by Clementine Beit

527. (*below*) *Arhai-din-ka-
Jhompra,* main entrance. *ca.*
A.D. 1200. Photograph by
Roderick Cameron